D1146538

YOUR
CONFIRMATION

YOUR
CONFIRMATION

John R. W. Stott

HODDER AND STOUGHTON
LONDON SYDNEY AUCKLAND TORONTO

ISBN 0 340 02829 7

Contents

Note. Where Biblical quotations depart from the Authorized Version, they are usually taken from the Revised Standard Version.

The Publishers are glad to commend to clergy, teachers, and all groups who use *Your Confirmation*, a set of six film-strips (330 frames in all) in full colour under the same title, illustrating in detail the teaching of each main section in this book. A descriptive brochure is available from many booksellers and visual-aid suppliers; or direct from the Church Pastoral-Aid Society, Falcon Court, 32 Fleet Street, London, E.C.4.

Introduction

CONFIRMATION is the first great milestone which a baptized and converted Christian passes on his pilgrimage to heaven. Outwardly it may seem just a memorable service in church; inwardly it can determine the whole course of your life. At your confirmation you are signing on for the Christian race. You are offering yourself in the service of Jesus Christ. Already at your baptism you were signed on your forehead with the sign of the cross in token that in later years you would "not be ashamed to confess the faith of Christ crucified and manfully to fight under His banner against sin, the world and the devil"; now at your confirmation you are yourself volunteering for the army of Christ, resolved to be His faithful soldier and servant to the end of your life.

Most people are confirmed in their teens. For them confirmation is their first responsible decision as they emerge out of childhood into independence. Others are confirmed in their twenties and thirties, and some later still. But whether you are young or old, confirmation has the same meaning and the same importance. It is much too solemn an occasion to be approached with anything less than sincere thoughtfulness. Every sensible person wants to prepare for his confirmation as carefully and as thoroughly as he can.

This book has three people in mind. First, there is the confirmation candidate who is still looking forward to his confirmation day. Secondly, there is the newly confirmed person who wants to think more about his recent confirmation and about the full Christian life on which he has embarked. Thirdly, there is the older and experienced Christian whose confirmation took place many years ago, whose memory of his pre-confirmation instruction has become rusty, and who feels the need of a simple refresher course on some Christian fundamentals. Perhaps I have tried to cram too much into a short compass. If so, forgive me. But Christians nowadays urgently need to have a firm grasp upon what they believe and how they should live. I am hopeful, therefore, that this brief manual may be thoughtfully pondered, and perhaps re-read each year at the time of your confirmation anniversary. It is good to take stock. It is so easy to slip back.

What, then, is the exact meaning of confirmation? The answer to this question is to be found in the two ways in which the verb "to confirm" is used in the Prayer Book. It is first used of your confirming, or renewing, the promises which were provisionally taken for you by your godparents at your baptism. It is then used of God who confirms, or strengthens, you through the laying-on of the Bishop's hands. The first use of the word indicates *your* part in the service; the second indicates *God's* part through the Bishop. We must now look at these two aspects of the service separately.

WHAT THE CANDIDATE DOES

Stated bluntly, the candidate declares in the service that he is now a real Christian, personally committed to the Lord Jesus Christ. I will suppose that you have been brought up in a Church of England home, and that you were baptized as a child.[1] You have now come to what the Prayer Book calls "the years of discretion". You can no longer rest under the umbrella of your god-

[1] If you are coming into the Church of England from another Church and were not baptized in infancy, some of this paragraph is not appropriate to you. But you will still in your confirmation publicly declare yourself a Christian, even if you had no godparents to promise this for you when you were a child.

parents. They cannot go on standing proxy for you. At your baptism they promised that you would renounce sin, trust in God and Jesus Christ, and obey His will in your life. That is to say, they promised that you would become a true Christian. The time has now come for you to make up your own mind. You can either repudiate what they promised in your name, or confirm it. You are old enough to decide thoughtfully and definitely that you want to follow Christ and belong to Him. But it is not enough to make this decision privately and secretly on your own. The Church gives you the opportunity publicly and openly, in the presence of God and before your family, your friends and the whole local congregation, to nail your colours to the mast and declare yourself to be now on the Lord's side.

Let me quote from the service itself. The preface explains the purpose of confirmation: "that children being now come to the years of discretion, and having learned what their godfathers and godmothers promised for them in baptism, they may themselves, with their own mouth and consent, openly before the Church, ratify and confirm the same". So the Bishop turns to the candidates and asks: "Do ye here, in the presence of God, and of this congregation, renew the solemn promise and vow that was made in your name at your baptism; ratifying and confirming the same in your own persons, and acknowledging yourselves bound to believe and to do all those things which your godfathers and godmothers then undertook for you?" [1] To that searching question the candidates together reply, "I do." Two monosyllables are sufficient to express the greatest decision any man, woman or child can ever make. You have submitted yourself to Jesus Christ.

[1] When the Confirmation Service from the 1928 Prayer Book is used, the Bishop may instead ask three separate questions based on the three baptismal promises.

You have said so publicly. This is the first meaning of confirmation.

WHAT GOD DOES

It is not until the candidates have made their tremendous declaration and the congregation have prayed for them, that they come in pairs to kneel before the Bishop. He lays his hands on them and says: "Defend, O Lord, this Thy child [or this Thy servant] with Thy heavenly grace, that he [she] may continue Thine for ever; and daily increase in Thy Holy Spirit more and more, until he [she] come unto Thy everlasting kingdom. Amen."

The laying-on of hands by the Bishop is the central act of the service. Indeed, the subtitle which the Prayer Book gives to the service is the "Laying-on of hands upon those that are baptized and come to years of discretion". To lay hands on somebody's head is a very ancient symbolical act, and it is used in four different ways in the Bible. First, it was a sign of general blessing. Jacob, shortly before his death, laid his hands on his two grandsons, Ephraim and Manasseh, praying that God would "bless the lads", and Jesus took the children "in His arms and blessed them, laying His hands upon them". Secondly, it was used in commissioning people for special tasks, and particularly in ordaining men to the ministry. The people of Israel laid their hands on the Levites, to dedicate them to the service of the tabernacle. Moses laid his hands on Joshua and commissioned him as his successor. The apostles laid their hands on the seven men who had been chosen to help them in the practical work of the Church; the Church of Antioch laid their hands on Barnabas and Saul when sending them off on the first missionary journey; and St. Paul and some "presbyters" laid their hands on Timothy, who was himself

to lay his hands on others. Thirdly, Jesus laid His
hands on the sick, sometimes on their head, and sometimes on the afflicted part of their body. Finally, there
was what we now call confirmation. When the first
Samaritans believed, the Jerusalem apostles sent Peter
and John to investigate. When they had satisfied themselves that they were genuine converts, they laid their
hands on them, as did St. Paul also on some Ephesian
disciples (who seem to have been followers of John the
Baptist) after he had baptized them in the name of the
Lord Jesus (Gen. 48: 14–16 and Mk. 10: 16; Num. 8:
10, 27: 15–23; Deut. 34: 9; Acts 6: 1–6, 13: 1–3; 1 Tim.
4: 14, 5: 22 and 2 Tim. 1: 6; Luke 4: 40; Acts 8: 14–
17 and 19: 1–7).

This act of laying hands on newly converted Christians does not seem to have been performed in every
case. They were all baptized; but they were probably
not all confirmed, unless the phrase "of the doctrine
of baptisms and of laying-on of hands" (Heb. 6: 2) be
pressed into making baptism and confirmation a universal practice. When a convert was baptized and confirmed, the one rite no doubt immediately followed the
other. As the years passed, however, and Christian
parents brought their children to baptism, confirmation
became gradually separated from baptism. Baptism
took place in infancy, but confirmation was reserved for
a later age when the candidate could speak for himself.

What, then, does the laying-on of hands signify?
The Bishop explains his own action in the collect which
follows the confirmation. He prays: "Almighty and
everlasting God . . . we make our humble supplica-
tions unto Thee for these Thy servants, upon whom
(after the example of Thy holy apostles) we have now
laid our hands, to certify them (by this sign) of Thy
favour and gracious goodness towards them. Let Thy
fatherly hand, we beseech Thee, ever be over them;
let Thy Holy Spirit ever be with them. . . ." The

laying-on of the Bishop's hands is here said to be a
certificate. It is a sign or pledge, certifying God's
favour and gracious goodness to the candidates. No
candidate receives this sign or certificate until he has
first publicly declared himself a repentant believer in
the Lord Jesus. First he has stood to bear his witness
to Christ; now he kneels to hear Christ's witness to
him. Has he accepted Christ? Then Christ has
accepted him. Has he confirmed his godparents'
promises? Then God has confirmed him, declaring
him to be in fact what he has already declared himself
to be. Has his own mouth borne testimony to Jesus
Christ? Then the Bishop's hand has borne testimony
to him that he is a child of God. Thus, the Bishop's
hand is but an earthly symbol of the fatherly hand of
God which will always guide and hold His children.

Neither the New Testament nor the Prayer Book
suggests that confirmation is the normal way to receive
the Holy Spirit. The Prayer Book service refers to the
candidates as the servants of God whom He has
already "vouchsafed to regenerate . . . by water and
the Holy Ghost", and the Bishop's prayer is that they
may "daily increase in" the Holy Spirit, not receive
Him for the first time. Certainly the candidates may
receive a special strengthening of the Holy Spirit.
For this we pray in the service: "Strengthen them, we
beseech Thee, O Lord, with the Holy Ghost the Comforter." Certainly, too, the Holy Spirit may be pleased
at confirmation to endow the candidate with some
special gift or gifts, as when Paul laid his hands on
Timothy (2 Tim. 1 : 6). We dare not limit the workings
of the Holy Spirit. It is clear in the New Testament
that on two occasions the Holy Spirit was given through
the laying-on of the hands of an apostle (Acts 8 : 14–17,
19 : 1–7), but these were special cases—the first Samari-
tan believers and some of John the Baptist's disciples.
They cannot be made the normal experience of first-

century Christians, and it is a safe principle of Biblical interpretation to begin with what is general and normal, not with what is special and abnormal. The general teaching of the New Testament is that we receive the Holy Spirit when we first hear the gospel, repent and believe in the Lord Jesus. This is what Paul calls "the hearing of faith". "Did you receive the Spirit by works of the law, or by hearing with faith?" he asks. We become the sons of God when we receive Jesus Christ into our lives, he further explains, and "because you are sons, God has sent the Spirit of His Son into our hearts" (Gal. 3: 2, 3: 26, 4: 6). Cornelius and his household received the Holy Spirit before they were baptized, let alone confirmed! (Acts 10: 44–48).

Here, then, is the double meaning of confirmation. It is an opportunity to confirm and to be confirmed; to declare yourself a Christian and to be declared a Christian. Thus confirmed, you are also a full member of the Church of England, ready to receive the privileges and assume the responsibilities of full Church membership which are described in the later pages of this book. But first, we must begin at the very beginning. If in being confirmed you state publicly that you are now by your own choice a Christian, and if through the laying-on of the Bishop's hands you are recognized as the Christian you profess to be, what is a Christian? The answer to this important question is the subject of the next chapter.

QUESTIONS FOR GROUP DISCUSSION

1. Can you put into vigorous modern English the three baptismal promises?
2. If we can accept Christ on our own, what is the purpose of confirmation?
3. How is the Holy Spirit received?

I

CHRISTIAN BEGINNINGS

How to Become a Christian

IN seeking to define precisely what a Christian is, it is unfortunately necessary to draw a distinction between being a "nominal" Christian on the one hand and being a "real" Christian on the other. It may seem invidious, and it is certainly distasteful, to have to distinguish, but in doing so we are only following the Biblical authors who lay much stress on the difference between outward profession and inward reality. It is possible to be a Christian in name without being a Christian in heart. This is particularly true in Great Britain. We live in a Christian country, whose laws and way of life have been profoundly influenced by Christianity; but to be a Briton is not to be a Christian. We may even have had the privileges of being brought up in a Christian home and receiving a Christian education; but to have Christian parents and Christian teachers, priceless advantage though it is, does not make anybody a Christian.

WHAT CHRISTIANITY IS NOT

So widespread is the ignorance, and so many are the misconceptions, of the Christian religion today, that I must begin rather negatively. It is often necessary to demolish before you can build. I am anxious to arrive at the centre of Christianity; I am not now concerned with the circumference. What is a Christian in essence?

First, to be a Christian is not just *to believe the*

Christian creed. Christianity is not in essence an intellectual system. It is neither a theology nor a philosophy. It is not a creed. To be a Christian is not just to give mental assent to a string of dogmas, however orthodox and true. You can recite the Apostles' Creed from beginning to end without any mental reservations and still not be a Christian. The best proof of what I am saying is the devil himself. He believes the creed. He knows it is true. But his belief does not make him Christian. As St. James wrote, "Even the demons believe—and shudder" (Jas. 2: 19). So if we are trusting in our orthodoxy of belief, we may be no better than demons!

Now do not misunderstand me. I am emphatically not saying that intellectual understanding is unimportant. On the contrary, it is vastly important. What I am saying is that it is not enough. By itself it does not make you a Christian. Christianity *has* a creed, a theology, a philosophy and dogmas; it *is* none of these things.

Secondly, to be a Christian is not just *to adopt the Christian code.* Some people think it is. Perhaps they go to the opposite extreme to the first category we have been considering. Thoughtless people often say: "It doesn't matter what you believe, so long as you lead a decent life." To them Christianity is just ethics. Now, Christianity has an ethic—indeed, the highest ethic the world has ever known, with its supreme law of love. You can, however, adopt Christian moral standards and strive to follow the Sermon on the Mount, and still not be a Christian. You can do this and be an agnostic, even an atheist. Mind you, if you are a Christian, you will lead a righteous life; but you can lead a righteous life and not be a Christian.

Thirdly, to be a Christian is not just *to undergo the Christian ceremonies.* Now, Christianity has ceremonies. The sacraments of Baptism and Holy Communion were instituted by Jesus and have been practised by the Christian Church ever since. They are both precious and profitable. This book is about confirmation, so that I shall not be thought to belittle this ordinance! Church membership and church attendance are an essential part of the Christian life; so are prayer and Bible-reading. These are some of the "observances" of a Christian, in public and in private, but he can engage in all these outward observances and miss the core of Christianity. The prophets were continually denouncing Israel and Judah for their empty ritual and vain religion, and Jesus condemned the Pharisees for the same sin.

WHAT CHRISTIANITY IS

If Christianity is in essence neither a creed, nor a code, nor ceremonies, what is it? It is Christ. Whoever first coined the phrase "Christianity is Christ" hit bedrock. "No other foundation can anyone lay than that which is laid," wrote St. Paul, "which is Jesus Christ" (1 Cor. 3:11). He is the foundation on which the superstructure of Christianity is built. He is the jewel which the casket of Christianity treasures. Christianity is not a system of any kind—philosophical, ethical or ceremonial; it is a Person. Take Christ from Christianity, and you murder it. Christianity without Christ is a dead and gruesome skeleton with neither flesh nor life. Once place Jesus Christ in the centre, and all other things follow—including both what you believe and how you behave. Dislodge Christ from His central position, and everything else is out of gear.

A Christian, then, is someone who is personally and decisively committed to Jesus Christ as his Saviour and his Lord. He has resolutely turned from his sins in repentance. He has trusted in the Lord Jesus as the One who loved him and gave Himself for him on the cross. He has surrendered his life to Him, promising to serve and obey Him in the fellowship of His Church. More briefly, he has repented, believed and surrendered. That this is relevant to our discussion should now be clear, since repentance, faith and surrender are the three baptismal promises which are renewed and ratified at confirmation.

COMMITMENT TO CHRIST

But how does one become committed to Jesus Christ? I want to suggest to you that there are four steps to be taken. They are simple to understand and easy to take, but they have far-reaching implications. To help fasten them in the memory, I will give you four words beginning with the letters A, B, C and D.

A stands for something to *Admit*. The first step is to admit that you are a sinner in God's sight and therefore need a Saviour from your sins. We are all sinners. The Bible says so. Experience confirms it. Not only have we broken God's laws; we have not even lived up to our own ideals. Our deeds and words may have been passable, but we would not like our friends to read our innermost thoughts and motives. In our better moments we are ashamed of ourselves. Now, part of the seriousness of our sins is that they have separated us from God. God is all-holy and absolutely pure. He hates sin. He cannot dwell with it. He cannot even look at it. He lives in unapproachable light. The darkness of our selfishness and sin cannot come anywhere near Him. We are cut off. So (in Biblical language) we need a Saviour. We need someone to build a bridge to span the gulf which separates us from God. Our bridges do not reach the other side. We cannot save ourselves. We must humbly and honestly admit this. Jesus said He had come to call not the righteous, but sinners. If, then, we are not sinners, or will not admit that we are, Jesus has no message for us.

B stands for something to *Believe*. We must believe that Jesus Christ is the Son of God who died on the cross to be the Saviour of the world. This is about all you need to believe in order to become a Christian. Of course there is much more to believe later. Once you are committed to Jesus Christ, you will be in a better position to think through the rest of the Christian creed, than if you remain uncommitted. You do not have to believe the whole Bible to become a Christian; nor to be well versed in the Christian philosophy of religion; nor to know the Catechism by heart! These things can wait. What you do have to believe is first that Jesus of Nazareth is the Son of God, uniquely divine, who came down from heaven and became man; and secondly that He deliberately went to the cross to die for the sins of the world. He bore them in His own body. He "was made sin for us". In His immense love for us He took upon Himself the penalty which our sins deserved.

You do not need fully to understand either of these two truths. The person and work of Jesus (the Incarnation and the Atonement, to give them their theological names) are two of the biggest mysteries of the Christian faith. We shall not fathom their depths till we get to heaven, if then. But you must believe the simple, straightforward facts of the gospel that Jesus is the Son of God, who died for you.

C stands for something to *Consider*. I want to ask you to consider that if you commit your life to Jesus Christ, He will be your Lord as well as your Saviour. He makes demands as well as offers. He offers you salvation; but He demands your thoughtful and total commitment. If you receive Christ, it will mean turning from everything you know to be wrong and submitting to the lordship of Christ. He will become master of your ambition and your career; master of your time, money and talents; master of every department of your life. We can escape neither repentance nor surrender. There is too much nominal, half-hearted, sentimental Christianity in the world. The momentous days in which we live call for our unconditional commitment to Jesus Christ. This is what He asked of His first disciples. This is what He asks of us. Nothing less will do. He told them, as He tells us, to count the cost of following Him.

D stands for something to *Do*. The first three steps have been in the mind, not the will. So far I have asked you to agree with three facts—that you are a sinner, that the divine Christ died for you, and that He wants to be your Lord as well as your Saviour. Not until now have you been asked to do anything. What is there to do? We may ask with the gaoler in the prison at Philippi: "What must I do to be saved?" The answer is that I must receive Jesus Christ personally as my Saviour and Lord. It is not enough to believe that He died to be the Saviour of the world and rose to be the Lord of the universe; I must ask Him to be *my* Saviour and *my* Lord. It is this act of personal commitment which so many people miss.

The verse which made it clear to me (nearly eighteen months *after* I had been confirmed, I am sorry to say) is a favourite with many Christians. It goes like this. "Behold, I stand at the door, and knock: if any man hear my voice, and open the door, I will come in to him, and will sup with him, and he with me" (Rev. 3: 20). In this verse Jesus pictures Himself as standing outside the closed door of our hearts and lives. He wants to come in. So He is knocking. And He promises that if we open the door, He will come in. Have you opened the door to Christ? Have you ever asked Him to come in? This is the essence of Christianity. It is tragically possible to be baptized and confirmed, to believe the creed and live an upright life, to go to church and to communion, to read the Bible and say your prayers, and still leave Christ outside the door. To open the door to Christ is in one act to fulfil the three promises your godparents made for you in baptism. It is to turn from your sins; to trust Christ as your Saviour; and to surrender to Him.

This is only a beginning; but it is an indispensable beginning. It is to this that you bear witness when you stand before the congregation on your confirmation day and, in answer to the Bishop's question, boldly say "I do." To be confirmed without having first accepted Christ personally is a mockery. I did not say you needed to know the date on which you took this step. Many do. Many do not. It does not matter. The real question is not *when* you opened the door to Christ, but *whether* you have ever done so. What makes me sure I am a Christian is not that I can look back to such and such a day and say "Then I accepted Him", but that *today* I can look into the face of Christ and say "Lord Jesus, Thou art my Saviour in whom I am trusting, and my Lord to whom I belong." Can you say that?

If not, I suggest that you need to take this step of receiving Christ. The last thing I want to do is to un-settle you unnecessarily. Yet my advice to you is: if you are not sure, make sure. This is too vital a matter to be uncertain about. It may be, as someone has said, that you are simply going over in ink what you have already written in pencil; but do not go on in doubt and indecision. Perhaps you would consider getting away and alone somewhere, and quietly echoing in your heart some such prayer as this:

"Lord Jesus Christ, I admit that I am a sinner. I have done, said and thought many wrong things. I turn from my sins in repentance.

"I thank Thee for dying for me; for bearing my sins in Thine own body; for taking the penalty my sins deserved.

"And now I open the door. Come in, Lord Jesus. Come in as my Saviour, to cleanse me. Come in as my Lord, to take control of me. And with Thy strength I will follow Thee and serve Thee, in fellowship with other Christians, all the days of my life. Amen."

QUESTIONS FOR GROUP DISCUSSION

1. "I believe in God and do no-one any harm." Why is this not enough?
2. What do you think are the greatest hindrances to becoming a Christian?
3. Is Christian conversion sudden or gradual?

How to be Sure you are a Christian

SUPPOSING you have opened the door of your soul and asked Jesus Christ to enter, can you be sure He has come in and forgiven you? You have accepted Him; but has He accepted you? It is one thing to be committed; it is another to be certain. Many people are content to hope for the best; they do not know for certain. Some folk go further, and say that you cannot know for certain. They even add that to say you know is to be guilty of pride and presumption. We must carefully examine this point of view.

Open the New Testament at random, and you will sense an atmosphere of quiet confidence and radiant assurance which is sadly lacking from many Christians today. The clear note of certainty rings and echoes through its pages. "I know whom I have believed, and am persuaded He is able to keep . . .," St. Paul boldly affirms. St. John even tells us that his main purpose in writing his first general epistle was to lead Christian believers into the certainty that they already possessed eternal life. "I write this to you who believe in the name of the Son of God," he says, "that you may know that you have eternal life" (2 Tim. 1: 12; 1 Jn. 5: 13). If God means us to have and enjoy eternal life while we are still on earth (and Jesus undoubtedly taught this), then He must mean us to know we have it, because we cannot enjoy something we do not know we possess. If a rich uncle were to transfer £500 to my bank account without telling me, and if I never bothered to look at my bank pass-sheets, my ignorance of his gift would make it impossible for me to use and enjoy it.

Not only does God want us to know we are in a right relationship with Him, but our peace of mind depends on it, and so does much of our ability to help other people. How can we show the way to others if we do not know it from personal experience ourselves? True, there are the dangers of spiritual pride and carelessness. There is the possibility that an assurance of our salvation may lead us either to adopt a superior attitude to others or to become smug and self-satisfied ourselves. But every right-minded person abominates these things, and the Bible gives no encouragement whatever to them. It is equally possible to have a deep certainty of acceptance before God and to remain both humble and zealous.

Assuming, then, that it is our Christian birthright not only to have eternal life, but also to know it, how can we come to this certainty? We learn from the Scriptures that there are three principal grounds for Christian assurance. They are rather like the three legs of a camera tripod. If the camera is to be steady, each of the three legs must be in use, secure and properly adjusted.

I. THE WORK OF GOD THE SON

The first ground of the Christian's assurance is the work of salvation which Jesus Christ, the Son of God, completed when He died on the cross. In order to explain this, I want to ask you a straight question: What is the object of your faith? If you are hoping that you are forgiven and that you are going to heaven when you die, in what are you trusting for these things? Think for a few moments. Re-read my question. Now, what is your answer? If you reply (as many people do to whom I have put this question): "Well, I have tried to lead a good life; I go to church regularly; I say my prayers; I . . ." I must stop you. You need go no further. The first word of your answer was "I". Exactly! You are trusting in yourself and in your own works, your good deeds and religious observances. No wonder you have no assurance of salvation! The answer to my question in one word is "Christ", or more elaborately: "I am trusting only in Jesus Christ who bore my sins on the cross. I have no hope of salvation except that He died for me."

> My hope is built on nothing less
> Than Jesu's blood and righteousness;
> I dare not trust the sweetest frame
> But wholly lean on Jesu's Name.
>> On Christ, the solid Rock, I stand;
>> All other ground is sinking sand.

St. Paul summed up this point when he wrote: "We [Christians] . . . glory in Christ Jesus, and put no confidence in the flesh [*that is*, in ourselves]" (Phil. 3: 3).

Perhaps you are beginning to see why the work of God the Son is the first ground of our assurance. It is for this reason. If you are trusting in yourself and your own works, they are not finished until you die; so you can never know if you have done enough. If, on the other hand, you are trusting in Jesus Christ and in His work on the cross, it was finished. When He had taken upon Himself the sins of the whole world, He cried, "It is finished." Then, since He "had offered for all time a single sacrifice for sins, He sat down at the right hand of God" (Jn. 19: 30; Heb. 10: 12).

This truth once broke into the mind of a young man of seventeen. His name was Hudson Taylor, and he was later to become a doctor and to found the well-known China Inland Mission. He was on holiday from work. His mother was away from home and (although he did not know this at the time) was praying earnestly for his conversion. He looked idly through his father's library and then picked up a tract and read it. I will let him tell the rest of the story in his own words:

"I . . . was struck with the phrase 'the finished work of Christ'. . . . Immediately the words 'It is finished' suggested themselves to my mind. What was finished? And I at once replied, 'A full and perfect atonement and satisfaction for sin. The debt was paid for our sins, and not for ours only, but also for the sins of the whole world.' Then came the further thought, 'If the whole work was finished and the whole debt paid, what is there left for me to do?' And with this dawned the joyful conviction, as light was flashed into my soul by the Holy Spirit, that there was nothing in the world to be done but to fall down on one's knees, and accepting this Saviour and His salvation praise Him for evermore." [1]

If, then, your conscience sometimes troubles you, and you feel burdened with guilt, and you wonder if you can ever have been cleansed and saved, turn away to the cross. To look in at yourself will confirm you in despair; but to look back to the Christ who died for you, and up to the Christ who reigns at the Father's right hand, will be to receive a hope which ripens into a joyful certainty. Never forget that our acceptance before God depends not on ourselves and what we can ever do, but on Christ and what He has done once and for all.

[1] "Hudson Taylor in Early Years", by Dr. and Mrs. Howard Taylor (1911), pp. 66–67.

2. THE WORD OF GOD THE FATHER

The first ground of the Christian's assurance is the finished work of God the Son. But how can we know that to trust in Christ and Him crucified brings forgiveness and eternal life? The answer to this is: Because God says so. The sure word of God the Father guarantees the finished work of God the Son. "If we receive the testimony of men, the testimony of God is greater; for this is the testimony of God that He has borne witness to His Son . . . he who has the Son has life; he who has not the Son of God has not life." This is what the Father has said about His Son. He has accepted His Son's sacrifice for our sins. He has shown His approval of it by raising Him from the dead and setting Him at His right hand in heaven. He promises to give eternal life to those who receive His Son. Now, where is the presumption? Is it presumptuous humbly and gratefully to believe God's word and be sure one has eternal life? I think not. Clearly the presumption is to doubt; it is sanity and wisdom and humility to believe, for "he who does not believe God, has made Him a liar, because he has not believed in the testimony that God has borne to His Son. And this is the testimony, that God gave us eternal life, and this life is in His Son" (1 Jn. 5:9–12).

I cannot emphasize too strongly that our certainty does *not* depend primarily on our feelings. Feelings are a bad index to our true spiritual condition. They are like the seesaw and the swings, up and down, to and fro. They rise and fall like a barometer. They ebb and flow like the tides of the sea. They are affected by our liver and kidneys and spleen; by the state of our bank balance and the nearness of our holidays; by our worries and responsibilities and problems. Read the

Bible and Christian biographies, and you will find that the saints have learned to mistrust their feelings. They have learned to trust God's promises instead. Feelings change; but the word of God abides for ever.

So make up your mind to learn by heart as many of the promises of God as you can find in Holy Scripture. Store them in your memory. Then when you get stuck in the bogs of doubt and depression, you will be able to haul yourself out by the ropes of divine promise. At the end of this chapter I have listed some of God's "exceeding great and precious promises" (2 Pet. 1 : 4). You might care to begin by committing these to memory. Then they will float into your mind when you need them, and you will be able to rest your soul and stay your mind upon them. We must learn to trust God's word. Whether we feel it is true or not does not affect its reliability one iota.

I want now to add something very important to what I have said about the sure word of God the Father. It is this. God has not given us a "naked" word to believe. He has "clothed" His promises. He has made them visible and tangible in what we call the sacraments. One of God's chief purposes in giving us the sacraments was to draw out and bolster up our poor, weak faith. He has given us promises enough in His word; but it is easier for us to lay hold of them when we see them dramatized before our eyes in the sacraments.

What is a sacrament? The Catechism defines it as "an outward and visible sign of an inward and spiritual grace given unto us, ordained by Christ Himself, as a means whereby we receive the same, and a pledge to assure us thereof". Some phrases of this definition we must leave for discussion in a later chapter. All we need here is the first phrase which I may perhaps paraphrase more simply by saying: "A sacrament is an outward and visible sign of an inward and spiritual gift of God." Similarly, one of the homilies calls sacraments "visible signs to which are annexed promises". God has not just given us promises; He has made His promises real and living to us by the outward and visible signs or sacraments called Baptism and Holy Communion.

We, too, use signs to convey more forcefully our promises. "I will forgive you all the past and be your friend," says a man to his former enemy, and holds out his hand as a token of his promise. "I love you and will be true to you for ever," says a husband to his wife, and covers her with kisses. His kisses demonstrate his love. "I will be loyal to my Queen and country," a soldier thinks in his heart as he gives a solemn salute. Our life is enriched by many such outward and visible signs. We pledge our friendship with a handshake, our love with a kiss, our loyalty with a salute.

In His loving understanding of our weakness, Almighty God has been pleased to do the same for us. The two great sacraments of the gospel, so called because they contain visible signs which picture the blessings of the gospel, are designed to awaken and deepen our dull and shallow faith. In baptism the outward and visible sign is water. It stands for the "heavenly washing", the inward cleansing through the blood of Christ, which we sinners need and which is offered to us in the gospel. An adult who has not been brought up in a Christian home and was not baptized in infancy repents and believes in Christ. He comes then to baptism. His baptism dramatizes his conversion. He himself publicly and openly declares the repentance, faith and surrender which he has already privately and secretly given to Jesus Christ. Then he is baptized. The minister applies water to his forehead in the name of the Trinity and declares him a born-again Christian. The sprinkling with water outwardly and visibly signifies the promise of cleansing which God has already given him in His word.[1]

Confirmation has the same meaning to an adult who was baptized in infancy as baptism has to an adult who was not baptized in infancy. Confirmation is not, strictly speaking, a sacrament of the gospel, because it was not instituted by Christ. Nevertheless it has an outward and visible sign. The laying-on of the hands of the Bishop has much the same meaning as the sprinkling of water by a minister. It represents outwardly and visibly that inward and invisible cleansing, and gift of the Spirit, which the candidate should already have received through his personal faith in Christ. God promises to give eternal life to those who trust in Christ; but He guarantees His promise by the signs of baptism and confirmation. The laying of the Bishop's hand on the candidate's head is the holding out of the hand of God to him in fatherly friendship. The sacraments are the kisses of His love.

In Holy Communion—the second of the two gospel sacraments—the outward and visible sign is bread and wine. These are tangible emblems of the death of Jesus. The bread is broken and the wine is poured out to exhibit the giving of His body and blood in death on the cross. Then the broken bread is eaten and the poured wine is drunk to indicate our personal share in what Christ has done for us.

"What happens to me if I sin?" asks a bewildered Christian. "Do I have to receive Christ all over again?" No, you do not. You were brought into acceptance with God (or "justified", as the Bible calls

[1] In the case of infant baptism the sprinkling of water is still a visible sign and seal. It pledges eternal life to the child and is therefore administered only after he has expressed (through the lips of his godparents) his repentance, faith and surrender. Its permanent validity depends on whether the child later accepts Christ and thus personally confirms the promises which his godparents took in his name.

it) once and for all when you received Christ. That is why you are baptized only once and confirmed once. At the same time, although we are justified only once, we need to be forgiven every day. That is why we come to Communion often. So if you fall, fall on your knees. Ask God's forgiveness at once. Do not wait till the next time you go to church. Do not even wait until your evening time of prayer. Confess your sin at once. Remember and claim God's wonderful promise: "If we confess our sins, God is faithful and just to forgive us our sins, and to cleanse us from all unrighteousness" (1 Jn. 1: 9). Then the bread and wine of Communion will give you repeated visible assurance of your forgiveness through Christ's death, as your baptism and confirmation assured you once and for all that you had been justified.

3. THE WITNESS OF GOD THE SPIRIT

I have urged you to mistrust your feelings because they fluctuate. Yet feelings have a place in the Christian's assurance—not the fickle flutters of a shallow emotion, but the steady increase of a deepening conviction. Of this the Bible speaks. It is the work of the Holy Spirit, who dwells in the inner sanctuary of a Christian's personality. There He is able to bear His strong but silent testimony to us. He pours God's love into our hearts, and He bears witness together with our spirit that we are God's children (Rom. 5: 5; 8: 15, 16). Do you sometimes become deeply aware that God is now your Father and you are His child? that the old tension between you is eased and the old friction gone? that you are right with Him and are living under His smile? that you are in vital relationship with Him when you seek Him in prayer? that His love enfolds and upholds you? This is the work of the Holy Spirit. He delights to assure you of these facts.

Do not rely too much on these evidences of God's for-giveness and favour. Thank Him for them when they come. But go on trusting Him if they are sometimes withdrawn.

The Holy Spirit bears witness to our Christian standing in another way, namely by the Christian char-acter which He is causing to develop in us. St. Paul called this "the fruit of the Spirit" which is "love, joy, peace, patience, kindness, goodness, faithfulness, gentle-ness, self-control" (Gal. 5: 22, 23). The Holy Spirit is a gardener, and His garden is our human life and character. If the garden is full of worthless weeds and poisonous plants, we may be sure that the Divine Gardener is absent from His garden. But if the lovely fruits of Christian holiness begin to appear, we may know that it is He who is causing them to grow and ripen. "You shall know them by their fruits," Jesus had said (Mt. 7: 16). Read St. John's first epistle some day at one sitting. You will notice what searching moral tests he applies to professing Christians. He makes it clear that if we are not walking in the light of righteous-ness, nor living a life of practical love towards our neigh-bours, we have certainly not been born of God. This then is the Holy Spirit's outward witness in our character which should corroborate His inward witness in our heart.

Such is God's loving concern that we should know we belong to Him, that each Person of the Holy Trinity has His part to play in giving us this certainty! The witness of God the Spirit confirms the word of God the Father concerning the work of God the Son. Let us be thankful that we can be so sure.

GOD'S PROMISES

Of Christ's acceptance of us   Rev. 3: 20; Jn. 6: 37.
Of eternal life   John 5:24;6:47;10:28.

Of daily forgiveness	I Jn. 1: 9.
Of Christ's abiding presence	Mt. 28: 20; Heb. 13: 5, 6.
Of divine wisdom	Jas. 1: 5.
Of strength in temptation	I Cor. 10: 13.
Of answered prayer	Jn. 15: 7.
Of peace of mind	Phil. 4: 6, 7.
Of God's faithfulness	Josh. 1: 9; Is. 41: 10.
Of God's guidance	Ps. 32: 8.
Of helping others	Jn. 7: 38.

QUESTIONS FOR GROUP DISCUSSION

1. Why is it important to know you are a Christian?
2. What place should "feelings" have in the Christian life?
3. How can the sacraments deepen our assurance of eternal life?

How to Grow as a Christian

O NE of the reasons why some people are reluctant to say they are sure they have eternal life is that they fear their assurance will lead them to stagnation. They imagine that once you are certain you have been reconciled to God, you will become smug and lazy, and lose all incentive to further activity. This is a shocking travesty of the truth and is due to a thorough misunderstanding of what the Bible teaches. How can it be supposed that once you know, you cease to grow? No such idea is to be found in the New Testament. The opposite is the case.

THE NEED TO GROW

The Scriptures draw a distinction between justification and sanctification, and every Christian should clearly grasp their meaning and their differences. "Justification" is the word which St. Paul uses to describe the position of acceptance with God into which a sinner is brought when he trusts in Christ as his Saviour. To "justify" is a legal term. It is borrowed from the law-courts. Its opposite is to condemn. It means to acquit, or to declare a prisoner just, not guilty. So the divine Judge, because His Son bore our condemnation, pronounces us righteous ("justifies" us) when we put our trust in Him. "There is now therefore no condemnation to them that are in Christ Jesus" (Rom. 8: 1). "Sanctification", on the other hand, is the word St. Paul and other apostles use to describe the purity of character which the indwelling Holy Spirit produces in the justified Christian. When God justifies us, He *declares* us righteous through Christ's death for us; when God sanctifies us, He *makes* us righteous through the Holy Spirit's power in us. Our justification concerns our outward position of acceptance; our sanctification concerns our inward holiness of character. The importance of this distinction here is that whereas our justification is sudden, our sanctification is gradual. It takes a few seconds in court for a judge to give sentence and for a prisoner to be acquitted. But it may take many years for a man's character to blossom.

The New Testament writers have another way of teaching the same truth. They say that when we commit ourselves to Jesus Christ as our Saviour and Lord, we are not only justified but regenerated or born again. The metaphor has changed. We have left the law-courts and entered the nursery. We see before us now not a prisoner who has been acquitted but a baby who has just been born. How long does it take for a baby to be born? Ask any mother or midwife. They will tell you. Not very long; only a few minutes. Months of preparation precede birth, but birth is a sudden and almost instantaneous crisis. A new, independent life emerges into the world. A baby who takes a few minutes to be born, however, takes a lifetime to grow. The years pass. He progresses from infancy to childhood, from childhood to adolescence, from adolescence to youth, from youth to middle age, from middle age to old age. The dramatic crisis of birth has been followed by the laborious process of growth. So what sanctification is to justification, growth is to birth. Justification and regeneration take place the moment a sinner is united to Jesus Christ by faith (whether he is conscious of that moment or not); sanctification and growth follow at a more leisurely pace.

Would that God would write this truth in the heart

of every reader, and burn it into his conscience! Our churches are full of Christians who were not only born again years ago, but who stopped growing years ago. This is a tragedy beyond description. God's purpose is that we should grow physically, mentally, emotionally and spiritually. It is a sad thing to be a dwarf and remain physically stunted. To be mentally backward is a great handicap, and to be retarded in emotional development leads to many problems. But the most pathetic state of all is that of arrested spiritual growth. Hundreds of Christians suffer from infantile regression of the spirit. They have never grown up. They have never graduated from the nursery. They are still what St. Paul dubbed "babes in Christ", whereas his ambition was to "present every man mature in Christ" (1 Cor. 3: 1; Col. 1: 28).

I want to appeal to you to take this matter seriously. It is a matter of pride to children to grow up. I can still remember the exultation I felt on the day I first got out of the pram and was allowed to walk; and my pride when I first exchanged shorts for long trousers knew no bounds! Then let us be equally keen to get out of our spiritual prams and shorts! Much depends on how you think about your confirmation. To some folk (especially young people) it is no more than an embarrassing ordeal they have got to get through somehow. That attitude is worse than useless. Better not be confirmed at all than think of it like that. Others are herded through confirmation at school like cattle through a gate, however much the school authorities try to avoid this state of affairs. Others take it thoughtfully enough at the time, but as soon as it is over they heave a sigh of relief, forget it as quickly as possible and concentrate on something else. One vicar has described how he walks through the streets of his parish and sees one of his former confirmation candidates lounging under every lamp-post. Others still continue their church membership. They get into the routine of saying their prayers and going to church. Outwardly they seem faithful enough. But inwardly they have dried up. Their spiritual life has withered like leaves in the autumn. They have stopped growing. They are almost defunct.

We ministers are often to blame, I know. Sometimes we do not take the trouble we should in preparing you for confirmation. At other times we set you a poor example. We also do not pray for you as we should. Whether you continue to grow or not depends also on you, however. I would urge you to make up your mind to regard your confirmation as a beginning, not an end; as the first milestone, not the last; as the gateway to a new life, not a cul-de-sac which leads nowhere. I expect you remember what Sir Winston Churchill said in November 1942, just after the successful conclusion of the Battle of El Alamein. Rommel and the Afrika Korps had been routed; 30,000 prisoners had been taken and the first great victory of the war had been won. Invited to attend the new Lord Mayor's luncheon banquet at the Mansion House, the Prime Minister said: "Gentlemen, this is not the end. It is not even the beginning of the end. But it is perhaps the end of the beginning." Loud cheers greeted his memorable statement. I hope that you will be just as enthusiastic in regarding your confirmation only as the end of the beginning, and as the prelude to further victories and greater exploits in the service of your Captain, Jesus Christ. Post-confirmation listlessness is a common malady; be on your guard against it. When your confirmation is behind you, it is no time to sit back and rest on your oars. It is time rather to press ahead with vigour and determination.

IN WHAT WAY WE SHOULD GROW

It is all very well to talk vaguely about the need to grow, but what is the meaning of Christian growth? The New Testament has a clear answer to this inquiry. It speaks of at least four different areas of progress.

First, we should *grow in faith.* Now, faith is an indispensable mark of the Christian. Again and again Christians are described as "believers", and Jesus called every follower of His "he that believeth in me". It is impossible to be a Christian without exercising faith. By faith we mean neither guesswork, nor credulity, nor superstition, nor making up what you know is not true. Faith is trust. The Christian is a believer because he has personally trusted in the Lord Jesus as his Saviour. He has handed himself over to Christ. So faith is confidence in Christ and dependence on Christ. It is also taking God at His word and believing His promises. All this may show why faith is essentially reasonable and sensible, because we are trusting a Person who is absolutely trustworthy. At the same time, when we begin the Christian life our faith is very small. Jesus needs often to refer to us as "O ye of little faith". Our faith is as tiny as a grain of mustard seed. We need to come to Christ, as the disciples did, and pray, "Lord, increase our faith". Then our worries will begin to dwindle and our fears to vanish away. As we meditate in the Bible on what God is like and on what God has said, our faith will mature, until perhaps it may be said of us, "Your faith is growing abundantly" (Mt. 8: 26; Luke 17: 5, 6; Rom. 10: 17; 2 Thess. 1: 3).

Secondly, we should *grow in love.* Jesus called His follower not only "he that believeth in me", but "he that loveth me". Love is the best of all Christian virtues. It is superior to faith and hope and knowledge. It is the greatest thing in the universe, because God is love. We are to love God, to love our neighbour and to love our Christian brethren. Love is one of the surest signs of Christian maturity. St. Paul knew at once that the Corinthian Christians were still spiritually childish because there was jealousy and strife among them. How few of us grow up in this way! We are suspicious of each other; we envy each other; we ignore each other. We are full of resentment and bitterness. We thirst for revenge on those who have hurt us. We have little sympathy and unselfishness. Would that Paul could write of us as he could of the Christians in Thessalonica: "The love of every one of you for one another is increasing"! Even then he would add: "We exhort you, brethren, to do so more and more" (Jn. 14: 21; 1 Cor. 3: 1–4; 2 Thess. 1: 3; 1 Thess. 4: 9, 10).

Thirdly, we should *grow in knowledge*. In these days, when many non-Christian philosophies and ideologies are abroad, it is essential for Christians to have an intelligent grasp of their faith. Too many Christians stop thinking. Do make sure that your intellectual understanding keeps pace with your devotional experience. When the heart is full and the head empty, dangerous fanaticisms arise. Yet when the Bible speaks of a growth in knowledge it does not just mean a dry, intellectual knowledge. Paul prayed that we might be "increasing in the knowledge of God", and Peter exhorted his readers to "grow in . . . the knowledge of our Lord and Saviour Jesus Christ" (Col. 1: 10; 2 Pet. 3: 18). The Christian life is fundamentally a personal friendship with God through Jesus Christ. Friendships are dynamic, living, growing relationships. They never stand still. They need to be cultivated and fostered. If you do not nurture them, they will go stale. So we must keep company with our Best Friend. Archbishop William Temple once said: "The loyalty of Christian youth is to Christ Himself. Nothing can take the place of the daily time of intimate companionship with the Lord; make time for it somehow, and secure that it is real."

Fourthly, we should *grow in holiness*. We have already thought a little about the process called sanctification. One of the most enlightening verses in the New Testament on this subject is 2 Corinthians 3: 18, where St. Paul asserts that Christians "are being changed into His (*that is*, Christ's) likeness from one degree of glory to another". Here is the Christian ideal. It is to become daily more like the Lord Jesus Himself. I love the chorus that children sing:

> Like Jesus, like Jesus,
> I want to be like Jesus;
>   I love Him so,
>   I want to grow
> Like Jesus day by day.

Again, it is a gradual process. "We beseech and exhort you in the Lord Jesus, that as you learned from us how you ought to live and to please God, just as you are doing, you do so more and more" (1 Thess. 4: 1). We do not become mature in the twinkling of an eye. Tempers are not tamed, nor passions controlled, nor selfishness conquered in a moment. Let the Divine Potter have His way, and He will fashion a beautiful vessel from the rough clay of our fallen nature. The Carpenter of Nazareth is still busy with His tools. Now by the chisel of pain, now by the hammer of affliction, now by the plane of adverse circumstance, He is creating an instrument of righteousness that He can use.

"O Jesus, Master-Carpenter of Nazareth, who on the cross through wood and nails hast wrought man's full salvation, wield well Thy tools in this Thy workshop, that we who come to Thee rough-hewn, may be fashioned into a truer beauty by Thy hand, who with the Father and the Holy Ghost livest and reignest, one God, world without end."

Be patient, but determined. Do not lose heart. Watch the discipline of your Christian life. Be diligent in prayer and Bible-reading, in church-going and attendance at the Lord's Supper. Make full use of your Sundays. Seek out Christian friends. Never leave your sins unconfessed and unforgiven. Never allow a pocket of resistance to arise in your heart. Above all, yield yourself without reserve to the power of the Holy Spirit who dwells within you. Then step by step you will advance along the road of holiness. Day by day you will grow towards full spiritual maturity.

BY WHAT MEANS WE MAY GROW

Part III of this book is devoted to a consideration of many of "the means of grace" by which a Christian grows. Here I will just anticipate briefly what I shall be elaborating later. How can Christian growth be ensured? If we take the analogy of a growing child (much used by the New Testament writers), we have our answer at once. Many factors combine to safeguard the healthy growth of a child, but two are more important than the rest. The greatest single condition of healthy physical growth is the regularity of a right diet. The greatest single condition of psychological growth is the security of a happy home. Each of these conditions has its parallel in the development of a "babe in Christ".

First, the right diet for a growing Christian is the word of God. "As newborn babes, desire the sincere milk of the word, that ye may grow thereby" (1 Pet. 2: 2). The Bible is the food of the soul. Many times it

likens itself to food. It is like honey because it is so
sweet to the taste. It contains both milk for the young
Christian and solid food for the more mature Christian.
We pray in our collect for the second Sunday in Advent
(often called "Bible Sunday"): "Blessed Lord, who
hast caused all holy Scriptures to be written for our
learning: Grant that we may . . . hear them, read,
mark, learn and inwardly digest them . . ." The so-
called Epistle of Barnabas, which abounds in quaint
and fanciful allegories, speaks of "those who know that
meditation is a work of gladness and who chew the cud
of the word of the Lord"! I shall have more practical
advice to give later about daily Bible-reading, but it is
not too early now to lay stress on the daily, dogged
discipline of it if we are ever to make progress and go
ahead with Christ. If the Bible is the Christian's food,
he will fall ill if he neglects it and starve if he ignores it
altogether.

Secondly, there is the security of a happy home.
Modern psychologists talk a great deal about the influence of our home surroundings on our early emotional development. God's wonderful plan is that little
children should be born into a family and grow up in a
secure and happy home. His purpose for the Christian
is the same. When we are born again, we are not born
in an isolation hospital! We are born into God's
family, the Church. God becomes our Heavenly
Father. The Lord Jesus becomes our Elder Brother,
and every other Christian in the world, whatever his
place or race, his nation or denomination, becomes our
brother or sister in Christ. If therefore a Christian
wants to grow up into healthy Christian maturity, he
can only do so in the family of God. Church membership is not a luxury; it is a duty. To try to dispense
with it is not only folly, but sin. Nobody has ever
developed into a balanced Christian who has not worshipped and (as the Americans say) "fellowshipped"

regularly with other Christians. Confirmation is the
door into full and active membership of the Church.

Here, then, is the secret of progress. If we want to
grow in faith and love, in knowledge and holiness, we
must seek the face of God every day in Bible-reading
and prayer and be drawn well and truly into the fellowship of the Church.

QUESTIONS FOR GROUP DISCUSSION

1. What are the marks of a mature Christian?
2. What do you consider to be the indispensable conditions
   of spiritual growth?
3. Look up Galatians 5: 16–26. What lessons on sanctification does this passage teach?

II

CHRISTIAN BELIEF

— 4 —

Belief in God the Father

WE turn now from Christian beginnings to Christian belief. We have already seen how important it is for a Christian to know what he believes and why he believes it. Indeed, the preface to the Confirmation Service says that "none hereafter shall be confirmed, but such as can say the Creed . . ." You do not actually have to say it in the service, but every Christian ought to know it by heart and have a good understanding of it too.

The word "creed" is derived from the Latin verb *credo*, I believe. The Creed in fact begins with these words. Christian creeds, then, are summaries of Christian belief, and people started making them at a very early date to help in the instruction of converts. There are even traces of short creeds in the New Testament (e.g. 1 Tim. 3 : 16).

Three creeds are included in our Book of Common Prayer.

1. *The Apostles' Creed*, which is said at Morning and Evening Prayer. It is to this that we usually refer when we talk simply of "the Creed". It was not composed by the twelve apostles and did not reach its present form until the middle of the eighth century A.D., but some of its clauses have been traced back to the second century. It is rightly called the Apostles' Creed because it states concisely the teaching which the apostles give us in the New Testament about God.

2. *The Nicene Creed*, which is said at Holy Communion. It is slightly longer than the Apostles' Creed.

49

It owes its name to the fact that it includes certain clauses about the deity of Jesus Christ which were agreed at the Council of Nicea in A.D. 325.

3. *The Creed of St. Athanasius*, which is also called *Quicunque Vult* from its opening words "Whosoever will" (be saved). It comes in the Prayer Book just after Morning and Evening Prayer. It is seldom used, although it is supposed to take the place of the Apostles' Creed at Morning Prayer on the Great Festivals and certain Saints' Days. It was not written by Athanasius, Bishop of Alexandria, at the beginning of the fourth century A.D., but is called after him because it emphasizes the full divinity of each Person of the Trinity just as he did in his great controversy with a presbyter of Alexandria called Arius, who denied the essential deity of Jesus. It probably dates from the fifth century A.D.

THE HOLY TRINITY

The Apostles' Creed and the Nicene Creed are divided into three paragraphs which concern the three Persons of the Trinity. The Catechism sums up the teaching of the Creed in the words:

"First, I learn to believe in God the Father, who hath made me, and all the world.

"Secondly, in God the Son, who hath redeemed me, and all mankind.

"Thirdly, in God the Holy Ghost, who sanctifieth me, and all the elect people of God."

Now, the Trinity is the biggest mystery of the Christian religion. The word itself is a contraction of the words "tri" and "unity", and refers to the fact that God is both three and one. To quote from Article I: "In unity of this Godhead there be three Persons, of one substance, power and eternity, the Father, the Son and the Holy Ghost."

Only two points need here be made about this doctrine, which is far beyond the grasp of our finite minds. First, the doctrine of the Trinity is not a peculiar theory invented by unpractical theologians; it is an attempt to put into words a truth which God revealed in facts of *history*. Let me explain. The apostles were Jews who had been brought up to believe in God, the Creator of the world and the Holy One of Israel. Then they met Jesus, and as they lived with Him, they came to realize that He was no mere man. He was divine. Yet He was not Himself the Father, for He used to pray to the Father. Then He started telling them of Someone else, whom He called "the Spirit of Truth" and "the Paraclete" or "Comforter", who would come and take His place when He had gone. On the Day of Pentecost this Holy Spirit did come with the fulness of divine power. But He was not the Father. Nor was He Jesus, who had now ascended to the Father's right hand. He was one with Them, and yet He was distinct from Them. So it was the pressure of their own experience which forced the apostles to believe in the Trinity.

Secondly, modern theologians [1] have shown that much of our difficulty in understanding the Trinity arises from confusion about the nature of unity. There are two kinds of unity which have been called "mathematical" and "organic". A mathematical unity is one and indivisible. An organic unity, on the other hand, may contain many component parts. Thus, when the atom was first discovered, scientists thought they had at last reached the basic unit of matter, only to discover that an atom is a little universe of its own. God's unity is organic also. He is One, but His unity comprehends the Father, the Son and the Holy Spirit.

[1] e.g. Professor Leonard Hodgson in "The Doctrine of the Trinity" (1943).

THE EXISTENCE OF GOD

This chapter is really about God the Father. The
Creed begins: "I believe in God". Like the Bible, the
Creed assumes the existence of God and does not argue
it. Ultimately, we have to accept God's existence by
faith rather than by proof because, being infinite, and
therefore beyond the reach of our finite minds, God
can only be known by His own revelation and not by
our unaided reason. I do not mean, however, that
belief in the existence of God is unreasonable. On the
contrary, there are sound reasons for believing that He
exists. There is no space here to elaborate the five
classical arguments for the existence of God which
were expounded by Thomas Aquinas. Perhaps instead
I may give just three lines of thought: [1]

1. *The fact of the universe*. All round us are pheno-
mena which are inexplicable apart from God. It is
reasonable to suppose that just as every building has
its architect, every painting its artist and every mechan-
ism its designer, so the universe, mysterious, beautiful
and intricate, must have had its Creator. He is the
Cause from which all effects ultimately derive. He is
the Life to which all life owes its being. He is the
Energy from which all motion comes. These thoughts
are expressed by the Biblical writers in various ways.
"The heavens are telling the glory of God, and the
firmament proclaims His handiwork." "Ever since
the creation of the world His invisible nature, namely,
His eternal power and deity, has been clearly per-
ceived in the things that have been made." "He Himself gives to all men life and breath and everything"
(Ps. 19: 1; Rom. 1: 20; Acts 17: 25).

2. *The nature of man*. If we look in at ourselves as

---

[1] You will find this whole question more fully treated in "Mere
Christianity", by C. S. Lewis.

well as out at the world, we find further evidence for the existence of God. High ideals and lofty aspirations stir within us. Things beautiful to our eyes and ears and touch deeply move us. Our mind is insatiably curious in its quest for knowledge. An imperious urge to do what we "ought" to do pulls us onward and upward, and burdens us with shame when we fail. Are these universal feelings an empty mockery, a mirage in the desert of illusion? Or is there some Ultimate Beauty, Truth and Goodness to which our whole human personality responds? More important still: what can be said of man's inborn reverence for high and holy things, his sense of awe and wonder, his craze to worship? Why is every man a worshipping creature, manufacturing his own god if none is revealed to him? Is there no God in whose service these longings can find their fulfilment? In the light of these facts of our own experience, it seems more reasonable to believe in God than to deny Him.

3. *The person of Jesus.* If God is infinite, He is beyond us. If He is beyond us, we cannot know Him unless He chooses to make Himself known. If He were to make Himself known, He would undoubtedly do so in the highest terms which would be intelligible to us, namely through human personality. It is exactly this that Christians believe He has done. God has not been content to reveal Himself merely in the universe He has made and in the nature He has given to man. He has come Himself into our world. In Jesus Christ He became man and lived among men. God made flesh was seen and heard and touched. The evidence for the deity of Jesus I must leave until the next chapter. It is enough here to say that the best and strongest argument for the existence of God is the Jesus of history. If by chance you are yourself doubtful about God, I urge you to read the gospels on your knees. "Seek and you will find," Jesus said. Come to

the historical records of Him who claimed to be the Son of the Father, with the open, humble, unprejudiced mind of a little child. It is to such that God reveals Himself.

GOD THE FATHER

The Apostles' Creed describes God as "the Father Almighty, Maker of heaven and earth". Here are three statements about God which we must briefly consider.

1. *The Creator.* The Nicene Creed adds that God is the Maker "of all things visible and invisible". This is clearly what the Bible teaches. "In the beginning God created the heavens and the earth"; ". . . the LORD made heaven and earth, the sea, and all that is in them"; "there is one God, the Father, from whom are all things" (Gen. 1: 1; Ex. 20: 11; 1 Cor. 8: 6). You will notice that in all these verses it is the *fact* of divine creation which is taught, and not the *mode*. The Bible tells us that God is the Creator of all things; it nowhere tells us how He did it. Many Christians today hold some form of the theory of evolution as an expression of God's creative activity, although it is clearly impossible for a Biblical Christian to hold a *mechanistic* view of the origin of life which virtually dispenses with God. Other Christians still believe in special creation, and particularly insist on the special creation of man, although most would agree that the six "days " of creation represent stages rather than precise periods of twenty-four hours, and would not want to press all the other details literally.

Much of the controversy about the first chapters of Genesis, and indeed of the debate between science and religion in general, has been quite unnecessary. Christians have themselves been open to blame by forgetting that the Bible was not designed by God to be a scientific textbook. Although no doubt the Bible contains some remarkable science, its purpose is religious, not scientific. God's word is designed to make us Christians, not scientists, and to lead us to eternal life through faith in Jesus Christ. It was not God's intention to reveal in Scripture what men could discover by their own investigations and experiments. So the first three chapters of Genesis reveal in particular four spiritual truths which could never be discovered by the scientific method. First, that God made everything. Secondly, that He made it out of nothing. There was no original raw material as eternal as Himself on which He could work. Thirdly, that He made man in His own image, able to think, to make responsible moral choices and to be related to Himself, which were all impossible for the animal creation. Fourthly, that everything which He made was "very good". When it left His hand it was perfect. Sin and suffering were foreign invasions into His lovely world, and spoiled what He had made.

2. *The Sustainer*. When the Creed speaks of "God the Father Almighty", it is referring not so much to His omnipotence as to His control over the things that He has made. What He created, He sustains. He is "the Maker and Preserver of all things both visible and invisible" (Article I). God did not wind up the universe like some clockwork toy and set it to run on its own. He did not just blow a whistle for the game to begin and then retire to the touchline to watch. No. He is "immanent" in His universe. He upholds, supervises and animates it and all creatures in it. I have no hesitation in saying that the dominant theme of the Bible is the sovereign, ceaseless activity of Almighty God. In contrast to the idols, which had eyes, ears, mouths and hands but could neither see nor hear, neither speak nor act, our God is a living and a busy God. In its own dramatic and figurative way the Bible leaves us in no doubt of this. The breath of all living

creatures is in His hand. The thunder is His voice and
the lightning His fire. He causes the sun to shine and
the rain to fall. He feeds the birds of the air and clothes
the lilies of the field. He makes the clouds His chariot
and the winds His messengers. He causes the grass to
grow. He stills the raging of the sea. He also guides
the affairs of men and nations. The mighty empires of
Assyria and Babylonia, of Egypt and Persia, of Greece
and Rome, were under His irresistible sway. He called
Abraham from Ur. He delivered the Israelites from
Egypt, led them across the wilderness and settled them
in the Promised Land. He gave them judges and kings,
priests and prophets. Finally He sent His only Son
through whom He established His kingdom in the
hearts of His people, which should extend to the utter-
most parts of the earth.

3. *The Father.* The Creed faithfully reflects the
Bible in holding together God's majesty and mercy,
His greatness and His goodness. He who is the
Creator of all men deigns to be the Father of those
who trust in Jesus Christ. Already in the Old Testament God was known as the Father of Israel, but when
Jesus came, the title became more personal and more
intimate. In His first recorded words as a boy of
twelve He spoke of His Father's business. In His last
words on the cross it was to the same Father that He
commended His spirit and died (Lk. 2: 49; 23: 46).
Not only did He Himself use this name for God, but
He taught us to do the same and when we pray to say
"Our Father who art in heaven" (Mt. 6: 9; cf. Lk. 11:
2). This is Christianity's distinctive title for God. It is
said that the Mohammedans have nearly one hundred
different names for God. They call Him "Creator,
Provider, Sustainer" and give Him many more designa-
tions, but not one of them is "Father".

God is not, however, the Father of all men indis-
criminately. Certainly He is the Creator of all. All

men are His "offspring" in the sense that they are His creatures. But the title "Father" was one which Jesus taught specially to His disciples, and both Paul and John make it clear that it is only through Christ the eternal Son of God that we can become sons of God and enter God's family. "To all who received Him (Jesus), who believed in His name, He gave power to become children of God", "for in Christ Jesus you are all sons of God, through faith" (Jn. 1: 12; Gal. 3: 26). The universal Fatherhood of God and the universal brotherhood of man, of which we hear much in these days, is potential, not actual. It cannot come until all men submit to Jesus Christ and receive Him.

It is hard to exaggerate the immense privileges we have once we are born again into God's family and become His children. "See what love the Father has given us, that we should be called children of God; and so we are" (1 Jn. 3: 1). We can now (and only now) really pray, because only now are we in relationship to Him. We can also enjoy perfect peace, as we trust in Him. With such a Father, how can we be afraid? "Do not be anxious," Jesus used to say—about your life, about your food and clothing, about tomorrow. "Your heavenly Father knows" was His antidote to worry (Mt. 6: 25-34, cf. v. 8). So it is our duty as well as our privilege to trust God. The son of God has no business to flap or to sulk. Doubt and discontent are unbecoming in the children of God. We must learn both to trust and obey this Father of infinite love, wisdom and power.

Perhaps "dependence" is the word with which we should leave this chapter. If God is our Creator and Sustainer, we depend upon Him as His creatures. If He is our heavenly Father, we depend upon Him as His children. We have two good reasons to look to Him with humble confidence. Let us glory in being the dependants of such a God.

QUESTIONS FOR GROUP DISCUSSION

1. "It does not matter what you believe, so long as you are sincere." Where is the fallacy here?
2. How would you seek to prove the existence of God to someone who is honestly inquiring, but has doubts?
3. What practical effect on us should our belief have that God is our Creator, Sustainer and Father?

Belief in Jesus Christ

As the first paragraph of the Creed concerns God the Father, the second paragraph concerns God the Son. It is longer than either the first paragraph or the third; but this will not surprise us when we remember, as we have already considered, that fundamentally Christianity is Christ. The Creed tells us both who Jesus Christ is and what He came into the world to do. That is, it describes His divine–human person and His saving work. These we must now study.

I. CHRIST'S PERSON, OR WHO HE IS

"I believe . . . in Jesus Christ His only Son our Lord . . . born of the Virgin Mary." This concise statement makes it clear that Jesus of Nazareth was both human, in that He was the son of Mary, and divine, in that He was the Son of God.

(a) *The humanity of Jesus*. The frank evidence of the gospels is that the carpenter-prophet from Nazareth of Galilee was truly man. He had a human body. It was born of a human mother and developed through adolescence to manhood as other bodies grow. He felt the pangs of hunger and thirst. The strain of His ceaseless ministry fatigued Him. He sat by the well-side to rest and fell asleep on a cushion in the boat. So gruelling was His agony in the garden of Gethsemane that His sweat, as it fell from Him, looked like great drops of blood. Finally, crucifixion killed Him. His dead body was lifted down by loving hands from the cross, bound in grave-clothes and laid in a rocky tomb. Not only was His body human, but He experienced human emotions too. He could look on a rich youth and love him. He could burst into tears at the graveside of Lazarus and weep again over the impenitent city of Jerusalem. Yet He could also rejoice, and often told people to be of good cheer. He felt compassion for the multitudes and turned on the Pharisees in anger for the stubbornness of their wicked heart. He also had a human spirit, which needed to maintain its fellowship with God in prayer, so that He was often out on the hillside communing with His Father in heaven. He was without any doubt "the man Christ Jesus".

(b) *The deity of Jesus.* But to say that Jesus was "born of the Virgin Mary" does not adequately explain Him. He was and is also God's "only Son". The Nicene Creed is fuller and describes Him as "the only-begotten Son of God, begotten of His Father before all worlds, God of God, Light of Light, very God of very God, begotten not made, being of one substance with the Father". Arius and his followers, whom I have already mentioned and who are usually called "Arians", taught that Jesus was a very superior, but a created, Being. After a long struggle and debate, which lasted many years, this doctrine was finally branded as heresy. The so-called Creed of St. Athanasius says that Jesus was "not made, nor created, but begotten". The significance of these words should be clear. You can make things out of various materials; you can create things out of nothing; but you can only "beget" children out of yourself. So Jesus was eternally begotten of the Father. He is "God of (*that is*, out of) God". Thus deriving His being from God, He is "of one substance with the Father".

So, although He was born into this world as other babies are born, He was conceived in the womb of

His mother as no other child has ever been conceived.
He had no earthly father. Instead, He was "con-
ceived by the Holy Ghost". The words of the angel
Gabriel to the Virgin Mary were: "The Holy Spirit
will come upon you, and the power of the Most High
will overshadow you; therefore the child to be born of
you will be called holy, the Son of God" (Lk. 1: 35).
Thus the Lord Jesus Christ "was incarnate by the Holy
Ghost of the Virgin Mary, and was made man" (Nicene
Creed). "Incarnate" means "clothed with flesh", and
what is called the doctrine of the Incarnation is the
Christian belief that in the womb of Mary God the Son
took human flesh and became man.

This is a tremendous claim. Unless we are so used to
it that we have become insensitive to it, it staggers the
mind and awes the spirit. Is this just a rather pic-
turesque fairy-tale? The pious fabrication of super-
stitious Christians? No! Can it really be true that
Jesus was God manifest in the flesh? Yes! There is
good evidence for it. In fact, so strong is the evidence
for the deity of Jesus that one cannot help wondering
if those who deny it have ever really investigated it.

Let us take the gospels as ordinary historical docu-
ments whose substantial reliability is not in dispute.
For the moment we can beg the question of their
inspiration. What do we find? We find a rustic
peasant-prophet from a very humble home in an
obscure village making such claims for Himself that
one begins to question His sanity. He calls the Eternal
God His Father. He presumes to say that the long-
expected kingdom of God is going to be inaugurated
by Him and that He is going to occupy the chief place
in it. He even calls God's kingdom "my kingdom".
He goes to the synagogue at Nazareth where He was
brought up, reads a passage from the prophecy of
Isaiah, and then has the effrontery to say that it refers
to Himself. Indeed, He asserts that all the sacred

Scriptures witness to Him and that He is their fulfilment. He calls Himself the light of the world and the
only way to God. He does not teach people to go to
God; He invites them to come to Him. Indeed, the
two are in His teaching the same thing. He dares to
forgive people's sins and brings on Himself the terrible
charge of blasphemy. Then He shocks His hearers by
saying that He is going to come back to judge the
world. The day of reckoning will be postponed until
His return. Then all the nations will be assembled
before His throne and He will settle the eternal
destiny of every individual sinner.

What can we make of these extravagant claims? He
advanced them with quiet, almost unassuming assurance. He was only a young man of barely thirty. He
had had very little education. He was a despised
Palestinian Jew. The Roman Emperor had almost
certainly never heard of Him. Yet repeatedly, con-
fidently, unostentatiously He made these stupendous
claims.

Was He mad? Had He what psychologists would
now call a megalomania? Was He suffering from a
fixed delusion about Himself? The strange thing is
that He reveals no traces of fanaticism or eccentricity.
The average, self-deluded person takes in nobody but
himself. Yet Jesus convinced many, and still convinces
millions today, because He seems to be what He
claimed to be. His character was consistent with His
claims. A man with delusions is obsessed with his own
importance. If he thinks he is somebody great, he
behaves like it. It is just here that Jesus confounds us.
Thinking Himself Somebody, He behaved like nobody.
Believing Himself to be God the Son, He could yet act
like a common slave, even an outcast. He took a towel
and a basin, and washed the feet of the twelve. He
made friends with publicans and harlots. He touched
lepers. He gave Himself away in the service of His

fellows. He yielded Himself to arrest and unjust trial. He made no attempt to resist when they mocked Him, flogged Him, spat at Him and crucified Him. He even prayed for the forgiveness of His tormentors.

Here is an inexplicable paradox—unless Jesus was the Son of God. It is this. In His words He was thoroughly self-centred; in His deeds He was thoroughly unself-centred. He advanced Himself in His teaching; in His behaviour He forgot Himself in the will of God and the welfare of men.

Add to this paradox His resurrection, and the evidence is complete. No satisfactory explanation of the disappearance of the body of Jesus from the tomb has ever been given except that God raised Him from the dead. Besides, the disciples were convinced. They affirmed dogmatically that they saw Him—several times and in different places. They were tough fishermen; they were not liable to hallucinations. And their subsequent behaviour proves the truth of their claim. They were changed men. No longer cowed and disillusioned and intimidated, they became fearless and vigorous preachers. They were willing even to hazard their lives for the name of the Lord Jesus. Nothing can adequately account for all this except that Jesus truly rose from the dead.

So He *was* the Son of God, as He was also the son of Mary. How can we reconcile these two truths? We cannot. The Creed makes no attempt to do so. The Creed of St. Athanasius wisely states both facts without trying to work them into a neat system. "Our Lord Jesus Christ, the Son of God," it says, "is God and Man; God, of the substance of the Father, begotten before the worlds; and Man, of the substance of His mother, born in the world, Perfect God and Perfect Man," "so that" (we may continue in the words of Article II) "two whole and perfect natures, that is to say, the Godhead and Manhood, were joined together

in One Person, never to be divided, whereof is one
Christ, very God, and very Man."

2. CHRIST'S WORK, OR WHAT HE DID

The Apostles' Creed passes straight from the birth
of Jesus to the death of Jesus. It says that He who
"was born of the Virgin Mary, suffered under Pontius
Pilate". It moves directly from the mother who bore
Him to the judge who condemned Him to death. The
reference to Pilate reminds us that the crucifixion of
Jesus is a historical fact which took place when the
notorious Pontius Pilate was procurator of the Roman
province of Judæa. Further, the immediate leap from
Christ's birth to His death reminds us that His death
is not just historical but central. It is scarcely an
exaggeration to say that He lived in order to die. His
death was (in His own language) the "hour" for which
He had come into the world and towards which He was
steadily and deliberately moving. When on His last
evening He instituted a supper by which His followers
were to commemorate Him, He gave them bread to
eat and wine to drink, which spoke to them neither of
His birth, nor His life, nor His teaching, nor His
miracles, but of His violent death on the cross. The
Church has always recognized the centrality of the
cross. It is not an accident that the cross is the symbol
of the Christian faith.

Then why did He die? The New Testament gives
many reasons for the death of Jesus. He died because
the accumulated forces of evil banded themselves together against Him. He died to prove that God's love
is inextinguishable and inexhaustible. He died to set
an everlasting example of how to bear undeserved
suffering with bravery and patience. But none of these
is the chief reason why He died. The Biblical authors
again and again link His death with our sins. This is

understandable because, as the Nicene Creed declares: it was "for us men and for our salvation" that He "came down from heaven". The Apostles' Creed is content to add that He "was crucified", but the Nicene Creed says that He "was crucified also *for us*".

To try to explain this, let me take two phrases from the first general epistle of St. Peter. He "Himself bore our sins in His body on the tree" and "Christ also died (or suffered) for sins once for all, the righteous for the unrighteous, that He might bring us to God" (1 Pet. 2: 24, 3: 18). On the cross Jesus identified Himself with our sins. He had already taken upon Him our flesh by His birth; now by His death He took upon Him our sin also. St. Paul could even say "He was made sin for us" (2 Cor. 5: 21). To "bear sin" is an Old Testament expression which means to endure the consequence of sin. So to say that He bore our sins is to say that He suffered the penalty which our sins deserved. Our sins contaminated and crushed Him. They came between Him and His Father until He cried, "My God, my God, why hast Thou forsaken me?" (Mt. 27: 46, quoted from Ps. 22: 1). This was no cry of human weakness wrung from His lips in despair. This was His own description in the very words of Scripture of the hell to which our sins had hounded Him.

> We may not know, we cannot tell,
>   What pains He had to bear;
> But we believe it was for us
>   He hung and suffered there.
>
> He died that we might be forgiven,
>   He died to make us good,
> That we might go at last to heaven,
>   Saved by His precious blood.
>
> There was no other good enough
>   To pay the price of sin,
> He only could unlock the gate
>   Of heaven, and let us in.

Only because Jesus bore in His own sacred and sinless body the foul sins of the whole world can any sinner ever be forgiven. God's righteousness has been perfectly satisfied. He has in His Son taken the judgment of our sins. He is Himself at once the Judge and the judged. No wonder the Creed ends with our belief "in the forgiveness of sins, the resurrection of the body and the life everlasting". Our forgiveness, our rising on the last day clothed in a new and glorious body, and our entrance into heaven to worship God in the life everlasting—all these are the "benefits of His passion". They would be impossible had our blessed Lord and Saviour not died for our sins. Well may we sing with the angels throughout eternity: "Worthy is the Lamb who was slain, to receive power and wealth and wisdom and might and honour and glory and blessing!" (Rev. 5: 12).

But the Creed does not end with Jesus on a cross. After describing His death, it mentions in rapid succession five other events in His saving career:

1. *He descended into hell.* The word for "hell" here could better be translated "paradise". It is not "gehenna", the place of punishment, but "hades", the place of departed spirits. The Lord told the penitent thief on the cross that he would be with Him that very day in paradise. The point of the inclusion of this sentence in the Creed is to show that Jesus, whose body died and was buried like other men, like other men also went in spirit to the next world.

2. *He rose again.* The chains of death could not bind Him. Death's prison could not hold him. He snapped the chains and broke from the prison, and emerged the glorious conqueror of death.

3. *He ascended into heaven.* After forty days, in which He kept appearing, disappearing and reappearing, He finally left His disciples. In His new resurrection body, which retained some identity with the old

body (in that He was still recognizable) and yet possessed wonderful new powers (He could pass through closed doors), He rose visibly from the ground and was exalted to heaven.

4. *He sits at God's right hand.* Since His work of redemption is completed, He is seated, and as a token of signal honour, it is at God's right hand that He sits.

5. *He shall come to judge the quick* (that is, the living) *and the dead.* Jesus Christ is coming back one day. He said so. There can be no doubt about it. But His second coming will be as triumphant as His first coming was lowly. "He shall come again *with glory*," says the Nicene Creed. At His return the day of judgment will take place. Those who have rejected Christ, the only Saviour, "shall suffer the punishment of eternal destruction and exclusion from the presence of the Lord and from the glory of His might" (2 Thess. 1 : 9); but those who have fled to Jesus for refuge from their sins and from God's wrath, will inherit His kingdom which "shall have no end" (Nicene Creed).

QUESTIONS FOR GROUP DISCUSSION

1. Supposing Jesus had been God in human disguise, and not truly man, how would it have mattered?
2. Can you list your reasons for believing that Jesus of Nazareth was the Son of God?
3. Study 2 Corinthians 5 : 14–21. What does this passage teach about the death of Jesus Christ?
4. What is Christ doing now?

—6—

Belief in the Holy Spirit

THE third paragraph of the Creed concerns the Holy Spirit. The Holy Spirit has sometimes been described as the neglected Person of the Trinity. I think this is true. Moreover, it is not surprising. The conception of God as our Heavenly Father is a natural and easy one. To visualize Jesus as He lived and died in Palestine is not difficult. But the Holy Spirit sounds so nebulous, so ethereal. It is much harder to grasp Him. The problem is not simplified by the unfortunate expression "Holy Ghost". I hope I do not have to tell you that the Holy Spirit has nothing whatever to do with ghosts! The word "ghost" is simply an old English word for spirit. You will even find several times in the Prayer Book the adjective "ghostly", meaning spiritual. He is called the Spirit because He is (like God the Father) a spiritual Being, who (unlike the Lord Jesus) has never had a body.

But He is God; and He is personal. First, He is God. The Apostles' Creed tells us practically nothing about Him. The Nicene Creed, however, describes Him as "the Lord . . . who proceedeth from the Father and the Son, who with the Father and the Son together is worshipped and glorified". He shares the sovereign lordship of God, and therefore deserves our worship and our praise. The Creed of St. Athanasius makes it quite clear that equal honour is due to each Person of the Trinity. "The Godhead of the Father, and of the Son, and of the Holy Ghost, is all one: the Glory equal, the Majesty co-eternal. . . . So the Father is God, the

68

Son is God, and the Holy Ghost is God. And yet They are not three Gods, but one God."

THE PERSONALITY OF THE HOLY SPIRIT

Secondly, the Holy Spirit is personal. Some Christians find this difficult to understand because the Holy Spirit never has had and never will have a body. But you can be personal without being corporeal! We ourselves after death and before the resurrection will be disembodied spirits, but we shall not cease to be personal.

There are two main reasons for knowing that the Holy Spirit is personal. To begin with, Jesus referred to Him as "He". In the Greek of St. John's Gospel the masculine pronoun is used of Him five times (Jn. 14: 26; 15: 26; 16: 8, 13, 14). This is the more striking when you remember that this masculine pronoun is in apposition to the noun for "Spirit", which is neuter. So the Holy Spirit is not a vague, indefinable influence, but a living Person. We must not insult Him by calling Him "it". The Spirit of God is a "He".[1]

The other reason for believing in the personality of the Holy Spirit is that the New Testament writers speak of Him as possessing both mind, feeling and will, which are the three commonly accepted constituents of personality. Thus, the phrase "the mind of the Spirit" occurs in Romans 8: 27, and He is said to exercise a number of functions, like searching, teaching and speaking, which are impossible without a mind. That He also has feeling is clear from Ephesians 4: 30, where we are told not to "grieve" Him by our sins.

[1] It is true that sometimes (e.g. Rom. 8: 16, 26) the Authorized Version has the phrase "the Spirit itself". This is because the reflexive pronoun is neuter like the Greek noun for "spirit". But the Revised Version rightly abandons grammatical accuracy for theological correctness and translates "the Spirit Himself".

The Greek verb here is used forty-two times in the New Testament and on each occasion of persons. You cannot grieve a thing or an influence. Only persons can feel sorrow. Thirdly, He has a will. St. Paul definitely states in 1 Corinthians 12: 11 that the sovereign Holy Spirit of God distributes spiritual gifts to different Christians "as He wills". He makes up His own mind. He chooses and decides. If, then, He has a mind with which to think, can feel sorrow and make decisions by His own will, we must conclude that He is fully personal.

THE WORK OF THE HOLY SPIRIT

The Holy Spirit is today the executive of the Godhead. Our present age is the dispensation of the Holy Spirit. If God the Father revealed Himself in the Old Testament, and Jesus Christ is portrayed in the gospels, the Acts of the Apostles are really the Acts of the Holy Spirit through the apostles, and the epistles disclose more of His work. The individual Christian's life and the life of the Church depend on the gracious presence and activity of the Holy Spirit. The three Creeds do not tell us much about His many functions, but I will attempt to make a summary of His work as it is described in the New Testament.

(a) *Christian conversion.* The experience of conversion is from first to last the work of the Holy Spirit. He is rightly called "the Spirit of grace" (Heb. 10: 29), because, like the Father and the Son, He yearns with undeserved love for the salvation of sinners. No man or woman has ever repented and turned to Jesus Christ but in answer to the loving appeals of the Holy Spirit. Thus, Jesus taught that it was the work of the Holy Spirit to "convince the world of sin and of righteousness and of judgment" (Jn. 16: 8-10). Every stab of conscience and pang of guilt, every longing for right relationship with God, and every anxious fear of coming judgment are prompted by Him. Next, He opens our blind eyes to see the glory and beauty and saving power of Jesus Christ. Preachers and writers may bear faithful testimony to Christ, but never a soul will be converted to Him unless the Holy Spirit adds His divine testimony. "He will bear witness to me," said Jesus (Jn. 15: 26). Once a sinner feels his sin and trusts the Saviour, he is born again; and the new birth also is the work of the Spirit. To be born again is to be "born of the Spirit" (Jn. 3: 6–8). It is He who imparts new life to the dead soul. No wonder the Nicene Creed calls Him "the Lord and giver of life". Notice how this phrase should read. It does not mean that He is "the Lord of life and the giver of life" (true as this is), but that He is "the Lord and the Lifegiver". He quickens into newness of life those who were dead in their trespasses and sins. In the next place, He "seals" the believer whom He has now entered (2 Cor. 1: 22; Eph. 1: 13; 4: 30). A seal is a mark of ownership. So God brands those who belong to Him. Their hallmark is the presence of the Holy Spirit in their hearts, for "anyone who does not have the Spirit of Christ does not belong to Him" (Rom. 8: 9). The Holy Spirit becomes therefore not only a "seal" but an "earnest" (2 Cor. 1: 22; Eph 1: 14). The Greek word here means a guarantee. He is the pledge of our future inheritance in heaven. Indeed, He is the first instalment of it. God has already, as it were, put down His deposit, as a token that the rest of what He has promised will in due course become ours. Finally, as we have already seen, the Holy Spirit bears "witness with our spirit that we are children of God" (Rom. 8: 16). So from beginning to end our conversion and regeneration are due to the influence of the Holy Spirit. He convicts of sin and reveals Christ. He enters our soul, quickens it to life, seals us as belonging to God, is the pledge and foretaste of the coming glory, and assures us within that we are God's children.

(b) *Christian holiness.* The Catechism is quite right to put into the mouth of the confirmation candidate the words: "I . . . believe . . . in God the Holy Ghost, who sanctifieth me, and all the elect people of God." The Creed does not mention that sanctification is the work of the Holy Spirit. But the Bible does. It is not in vain that He is called the *Holy* Spirit, for it is He who produces holiness in the people of God. I have already written about Him as the Divine Gardener who causes righteousness to ripen like fruit in our lives. It is by His inward power that our evil desires can be controlled and our strong passions tamed. "Walk in the Spirit," wrote St. Paul just before describing the Spirit's lovely fruit, "and you will not fulfil (or gratify) the desires of the flesh" (Gal. 5: 16). To "walk in the Spirit" means to live each moment under the dominion of the Spirit and remain surrendered to His authority and power. Here is the greatest single secret of holiness which the New Testament reveals. It is not to strive to live like Christ, but to let Christ by His Spirit live and reign in us. We need urgently to heed Paul's command: "Be filled with the Spirit" (Eph 5: 18). The tense is a present imperative passive. It means: "Go on being filled" or "Continue to be filled". The Christian life is not to be lived by fits and starts, but by a continuous and growing experience of the fulness of the Holy Spirit.

(c) *Christian understanding.* The Nicene Creed includes the significant phrase that the Holy Spirit "spake by the prophets". I shall be writing in Chapter 8 about the inspiration of the Bible. Suffice it to say here that the Creed affirms (what the Scriptures teach) that the prophets were the vehicle of the Holy Spirit's revelation. He spoke through them, so that their words were His words. What is true of the Old Testament prophets is true also of the New Testament apostles. That is why we call the Bible "the word of God". He is the primary author of it by His Spirit. Now, if He is the original author of the Bible, He is obviously also its best interpreter. It is not enough that He caused it to be written. We need Him to illumine our minds to understand it. Daily Bible-reading is an almost worthless routine unless He opens our eyes to see its meaning and its application. I suggest you learn by heart the Psalmist's prayer, and repeat it before ever you read from God's word: "Open Thou mine eyes, that I may behold wondrous things out of Thy law" (Ps. 119: 18). Have you a sundial in your garden? Then try to tell the time from it on a dull and cloudy day. You cannot. It is impossible. All you see is figures, with no message. But let the sun break through the clouds and shine on the dial, and the finger immediately points its message for you to read. So, too, only the Spirit of truth can transform the letters and words and sentences of the Book of God into a personal message to our hearts.

(d) *Christian fellowship*. It is important to notice that the Creed passes immediately from "I believe in the Holy Ghost" to "the holy, catholic Church"; because the Spirit of God is the creator of the Church of God. The Church of Christ was born on the Day of Pentecost when the Holy Spirit came from heaven and a group of individuals were spiritually united into one fellowship. The Church is essentially a fellowship, a *koinonia*. This word means literally "a common sharing in"; and it is our common participation in the Holy Spirit which makes us one. If He dwells in you and if He dwells in me, then we are united by Him. We may never have met. We may never even have heard of each other, but He has joined us together. The Church is "the fellowship of the Spirit". St. Paul again and again refers to this truth. "There is one body and one Spirit," he writes to the Ephesians (Eph. 4: 4). Indeed, he might have said, "there is one body *because* there is one Spirit". It is the one Spirit who creates the one body. The body is the body of Christ, the Church. It is not divided. It cannot be. Even our outward divisions do not tear it asunder, for the one Spirit animates it. Piers in a harbour may divide it into sections, so that boats are cut off from each other, but the same sea flows and swells beneath them. Our man-made denominations may outwardly and visibly separate us from one another, but inwardly and invisibly the tide of the Spirit unites us. The Church is called in the Communion Service "the blessed company of all faithful [that is, believing] people". Every true believer in Jesus Christ is a member of the Church of Christ, whatever his nation or denomination, his race or rank, his age or sex. This is the "Holy, Catholic Church". The word "catholic" simply means universal, and the one omnipresent Spirit makes the universal Church one. Not even death can separate us from one another. "The communion of saints" means that the Church militant on earth and the Church triumphant in heaven, even if they cannot actively commune with one another, are still united in Christ by the Spirit.

(e) *Christian service.* The Holy Spirit is concerned not only to unite the Church, but to convert the world. It is His desire not only to fill the Christian but to overflow from him into the lives of others. Jesus promised that from the innermost being of the Christian believer "rivers of living water" would flow, referring to the Holy Spirit (Jn. 7: 37–39). True, the Holy Spirit endows different Christians with different gifts, just as one body has many different members, each with a different function (1 Cor. 12). At the same time every Christian is called to be a witness to Jesus Christ, and the whole Church is committed to worldwide evangelism; but all witness is empty talk and all evangelism ineffective without the dynamic power of the Holy Spirit. Read the Acts and see what He did in olden days through ordinary lives surrendered to Him! He gave boldness to timid fishermen; He took their feeble, stammering words and confirmed them with irresistible force in the conscience of the hearers (Acts 4: 31; 2: 37–41). Paul himself for all the power of his intellect is thought to have been ugly in appearance and slow of speech. His critics said of him that his bodily presence was weak and his speech contemptible (2 Cor. 10: 10). It is no surprise then to learn from him that when he visited people "in weakness and much fear and trembling", he relied not on "plausible words of wisdom", but on the "demonstration of the Spirit and power" (1 Cor. 2: 3, 4; cf. 1 Thess. 1: 5). He might stutter words of great human weakness; but the Holy Spirit would "demonstrate" them to his listeners with divine power. What was true of Paul must needs be true of every Christian worker today, whether in the ministry or out of it. What we need is not more learning, not more eloquence, not more persuasion, not more organization, but more power from the Holy Spirit. The word of Jesus is directed to each of us. "You shall receive power when the Holy Spirit has come upon you; and you shall be my witnesses" (Acts 1: 8). Do you want to be His witness? Then you must have His power. Do you want His power? Then you must have His Spirit.

There is perhaps no greater need in the Church of God today than that we should be filled with the Holy Spirit; that He should convert us, sanctify us, teach us, unite us, and use us; and that we should "evermore . . . rejoice in His holy comfort".[1]

[1] Collect for Whitsunday.

QUESTIONS FOR GROUP DISCUSSION

1. How do we know that the Holy Spirit is personal?
2. What does the Bible reveal of the Holy Spirit's work before Pentecost?
3. How would you say we need the Holy Spirit most today?
4. What is the Church?

III

CHRISTIAN BEHAVIOUR

7

Holiness of Life

WE turn from Christian belief to Christian behaviour.

The Christian life is a holy life. Nobody can read
the Bible and miss this. If we are Christians, we have
been called "with a holy calling". God the Father
"chose us . . . before the foundation of the world,
that we should be holy and blameless before Him".
The Lord Jesus died for us not only that we might be
forgiven, but that He might "redeem us from all
iniquity and . . . purify to Himself a people of His own
who are zealous for good deeds". The Holy Spirit
dwells within us in order to sanctify us. Thus each
Person of the Trinity is actively concerned for our
holiness. "You shall be holy, for I am holy," God says
(2 Tim. 1: 9; Eph. 1: 4; Tit. 2: 14; 1 Thess. 4: 7, 8;
1 Pet. 1 : 16, quoted from Lev. 11 : 44, 45).

The ten commandments are still the basic standard
for holy living. They are not just the laws of Moses,
but the law of God. They are still in force today, not
that by obeying them we may win salvation, but that,
having been saved, we may know how to live a life
that is pleasing to God. Jesus summarized the teaching
of the ten commandments by the supreme law of love.
He brought together two verses from the Old Testament and said: "You shall love the Lord your God with
all your heart, and with all your soul, and with all your
mind. This is the great and first commandment. And
a second is like it, You shall love your neighbour as
yourself. On these two commandments depend all the
law and the prophets" (Deut. 6: 5; Lev. 19: 18; Mt.

22: 37–40). The ten commandments are mostly negative, "thou shalt not"; the summary of Jesus is positive, "thou shalt love". The ten commandments are a catalogue of precepts; the summary of Jesus is one comprehensive principle, love. The love which Jesus meant is neither sloppy, nor sentimental, nor selfish. It is strong, robust and sacrificial. What men often call love is in reality only a desire to get and to possess; what the Bible means by love is the desire to give and to enrich. "God so loved the world that He gave His only Son." "The Son of God loved me and gave Himself for me" (Jn. 3: 16; Gal. 2: 20). For us too loving will involve selfgiving. Truly to love God is to be absorbed in His will and in His glory, not our own. Truly to love men is to be engrossed in their welfare, not our own. The ten commandments show us how this principle operates in practice.

OUR DUTY TO GOD

The first five commandments concern our duty to God.

1. *You shall have no other gods besides me.* This is God's demand for our exclusive worship. We are to put Him first in every department of our lives. The question is not what I want, but what will most promote His glory and conform to His will.

2. *You shall not make yourself a graven image.* If the first commandment requires our exclusive worship, the second demands that it shall be spiritual. "God is spirit, and those who worship Him must worship in spirit," Jesus said (Jn. 4: 24). Whatever outward forms we may employ to help or to express our worship, the worship that is pleasing to God is in essence the inner devotion of our hearts. For this He is "jealous". He has the right to demand our undivided, single-minded allegiance; for He is God, and there is no other. The reference to "visiting the iniquity of the fathers upon

the children" reminds us that we cannot keep the results of our sins to ourselves. The sins of parents can still be transmitted to their children—physically (by inherited disease), socially (e.g. in the poverty caused by drunkenness or gambling), psychologically (by the tensions and conflicts of an unhappy home) and morally (in habits learned from a bad example).

3. *You shall not take the name of the Lord your God in vain.* Every Christian needs to watch his vocabulary. Bad language, swearing and particularly the profane use of God's name are dishonouring to Him. We also take His name in vain by our hypocrisies, when we call God one thing in our prayers and contradict it in our daily lives, and by taking solemn oaths in His name which we fail to keep.

4. *Remember the sabbath day, to keep it holy.*[1] Sunday is "the Lord's Day", and not our day. The Christian spends it, therefore, not just to please himself, but in the way that God intended. Jesus made it plain that "the sabbath was made for man" (Mk. 2: 27). It was designed to give man's body and mind the chance to rest, and his spirit the chance to worship. We all need one day's rest in seven; and church attendance is a definite Christian duty on Sundays. We should also make sure that our Sunday activities do not deny rest and worship to *others*.

5. *Honour your father and your mother.* This commandment belongs to the first table of the law (dealing with our duty to God) probably because until we come of age our parents stand to us *in loco dei*. They represent to us God's authority. The Catechism is right therefore to extend this law to include our duty to the Queen and all in authority under her, and to all our "governors, teachers, spiritual pastors and masters".

[1] The Jewish observance of the sabbath (the seventh day) was changed by the early Christians into an observance of the first day of the week, to commemorate the Resurrection.

Our behaviour towards them often betrays our real attitude towards God.

OUR DUTY TO MAN

Our duty to our neighbour is summed up in the golden rule: "Whatever you wish that men should do to you, do so to them" (Mt. 7: 12). In the words of the Catechism it is "to hurt nobody by word nor deed", for, as St. Paul wrote: "Love does no wrong to a neighbour; therefore love is the fulfilling of the law" (Rom. 13: 8–10). If we truly love other men, we shall respect their rights and desire their good. The remaining commandments enumerate five offences against love.

6. *You shall not kill.* A man's life is his most precious possession, so that to rob him of it is the first and greatest denial of love. Moreover, Jesus taught in the Sermon on the Mount that God takes into account our thoughts as well as our deeds (Mt. 5: 21, 22). It is possible to commit murder by cruel words and angry looks as well as by a dagger or a gun. In the sight of God we break this commandment when we lose our temper and hate other people in our hearts.

7. *You shall not commit adultery.* Strictly speaking, adultery is sexual intercourse between *married* people (other than husband and wife). Its wickedness is increased because it drags into the mud the holy estate of marriage, which God Himself instituted and which He meant to be a permanent bond of love, reflecting the love between Christ and His Church (Eph. 5: 21–33). Adultery breaks up homes and damages the healthy development of children. But this commandment also forbids all kinds of impurity, which is the acme of selfishness. Sex is a precious gift of God, to be used and enjoyed in its proper place and time, which is in marriage. The Christian's body is the temple in which the Holy Spirit dwells. He must learn to keep it "in temperance, soberness and chastity" (Catechism), and to control his thoughts.

8. *You shall not steal.* This commandment covers more than theft. It includes all dishonesty and cheating, all underhand intrigue, tax evasion and dodging the Customs. It implies too as its positive counterpart: "to learn and labour to get mine own living" (Catechism).

9. *You shall not bear false witness.* The Christian is honest in word as well as deed. His word can be trusted. Lies and subterfuges are abhorrent to him. He knows the power of the tongue for good or evil, and he seeks the grace of God to bridle it (see Ps. 141: 3; Jas. 1: 26 and 3: 1–12). He is guilty neither of perjury, nor of malicious gossip, nor of slander. He does not talk behind the other fellow's back.

10. *You shall not covet.* This important last command transforms the decalogue from an outward civil code into an inward moral law. You cannot be had up in the courts for covetousness, for covetousness is neither an act nor a word, but a disposition of heart. Covetousness is in fact to stealing what lust is to adultery and what angry thoughts are to murder. The law of the land is not concerned about our thoughts and motives; but God is. Covetousness is idolatry, He says (Eph. 5: 5). It is a sin not only against man, but Himself. It is to allow some thing or person to usurp the chief place in one's affections and desires. The contrary Christian virtue is contentment, "for He has said 'I will never fail you nor forsake you'" (Heb. 13: 5).

THE WAY OF HOLINESS

Such a high standard of morality might well drive us to despair. Well does the Catechism continue: "My good child, know this, that thou art not able to do these things of thyself." How, then, can we keep these commandments and live this life of love to God and man? The Bible indicates two ways:

1. *Faith.* Faith is a receptive quality. It is the open

hand which receives the grace of God. Power to lead a holy life is in the Holy Spirit. We have seen already the need to keep our will surrendered to Him, and by faith every day, and many times during each day, to ask Him to fill us with Himself. Then He will subdue our passions and produce in our lives His lovely fruit.

2. *Discipline.* Granted that the grace or power of God alone can sanctify us, there are various ways through which His strength can reach us. These are usually called "the means of grace" because they are channels through which God's power can come to us. One is prayer; another is the Bible. A third is the Holy Communion service. Christian worship and fellowship are others. If we are not diligent in our use of these "means of grace", we shall definitely not grow in holiness. As one writer has put it, there are "no gains without pains" in the Christian life. If you want to be slack, don't expect to be holy! The best way to resist germs is not to take patent medicines when an epidemic breaks out, but to build up your resistance to disease the whole of the year. So, too, the secret of overcoming temptation is not in what you do at the moment of the assault (important as it is then to look to the Lord Jesus for His power). It is rather to build up your spiritual strength all the time by the discipline of your Christian life.

To the "means of grace" we now turn.

QUESTIONS FOR GROUP DISCUSSION

1. Henry Drummond called love "the greatest thing in the world". What made him say this?
2. "The ten commandments are old-fashioned and out-of-date." Discuss this opinion.
3. Somebody says: "However hard I try, I can't overcome my besetting sins." What advice would you give to this person?

8

Bible-reading and Prayer

IF you want to make steady progress in the Christian life, nothing is more important than daily "quiet times" with God. You will never grow unless you make time for this. This is the resolute discipline of the Christian life. First thing in the morning and last thing at night you have a sacred engagement with God. Persevere in it, and soon you will have formed a habit which nothing but illness can break.

If these times of quiet waiting upon God are to be balanced, they will consist of Bible-reading and prayer —and in that order. First, let God speak to you through His word. Then speak back to God in prayer. It is like the swing of a pendulum. It is a two-way conversation.

I. BIBLE-READING

The reason why we must regularly read the Bible is because it is God's word, through which He can make Himself known to us today. Two questions confront us now: first, why do we believe it to be God's word? Secondly, how we should read it?

(a) *Why to believe the Bible*. We must begin by realizing that the idea of revelation is fundamentally reasonable. Revelation means "unveiling". Before revelation God is veiled. His nature, character and purposes are hidden from us. We cannot see Him. He is invisible and unapproachable. How can our little minds reach or fathom the thoughts of the infinite mind of Almighty God? It is impossible. "My thoughts are not your thoughts, neither are your ways my ways, says the Lord. For as the heavens are higher than the earth, so are my ways higher than your ways and my thoughts than your thoughts" (Is. 55 : 8, 9). If we are to know God at all, He must take the initiative and disclose Himself to us; we cannot discover Him by ourselves. If we are ever to understand what goes on in the mind of God, He must speak, so that we can learn His thoughts from His words.

It is exactly this that God has done, and what He has revealed and said is faithfully recorded in the Bible. Over a long period of time and progressively, He made Himself known to the patriarchs, to Israel and finally in Christ and to the apostles of Christ. Again and again the prophets began their oracles: "The word of the Lord came unto me, saying" or "Thus saith the Lord" or "Hear the word of the Lord". Jesus Himself absolutely trusted these Old Testament Scriptures. He reverently obeyed them. He believed that they were fulfilled in Himself. He quoted them as His authority when debating with His critics. He said: "The Scripture cannot be broken" (Jn. 10 : 35). We must then be careful not to have a smaller regard for their authority and value than He had. The New Testament writers had the same respect for the Old Testament. Many times they quote from it. Paul wrote: "All scripture is given by inspiration of God" (literally, "God-breathed"), and Peter explained: "No prophecy ever came by the impulse of man, but men spoke from God as they were moved by the Holy Spirit" (2 Tim. 3 : 16; 2 Pet. 1 : 21).

Jesus not only believed the Old Testament; He clearly anticipated the writing of the New. He promised that when the Holy Spirit had come, He would bring to the remembrance of the apostles all that He had taught them, would lead them into all the truth and would declare to them the things that were to come (Jn. 14: 26; 16: 12, 13). These promises were fulfilled in the writing of the gospels, the epistles and the Revelation.

Moreover, the Bible wonderfully seems to be what it claims to be. Every reader is impressed by the unity of its theme, when he remembers that it took about fifteen hundred years to write, contains sixty-six different books and that some forty authors had a hand in its composition. Its prophecies have been remarkably fulfilled. Its doctrines are noble and its ethics lofty. Nearly two thousand years after Christ its popularity continues to increase. It has brought salvation to sinners and encouragement to saints, guidance to the perplexed, comfort to the dying and hope to the be-reaved. Every man who reads it with an open mind and a humble spirit testifies to its power both to hurt and to heal. As the Chinese Christian said to a missionary: "Every time I read that Book, it kicks me!" The final proof that it is the word of God is that God speaks through its pages to my own soul.

I do not mean that it is all equally profitable; nor that it is all easy to understand. Great care is needed in interpreting it. The reader has to remember that many kinds of literature are found in it. Some is prose and some poetry. Some is literal and some figurative. Some is history and some prophecy. Each part must be interpreted according to its character. Again, no passage of Scripture is fully intelligible on its own. It is never safe to isolate verses, chapters or even books. The text must be read in the light of the context, and each must be understood in the light of all.

(b) *How to read the Bible*. Method is essential. I urge you to be systematic. Abandon the dabster method for good and all! Don't imitate the butterfly, which flits irresponsibly from flower to flower! The two best-known systems of daily Bible-reading are the

Scripture Union and the Bible-Reading Fellowship.[1]
If you have no method of your own, I strongly recom-
mend you to join one of these. Both have graded
explanatory notes to suit your age and experience. If
in the morning you read the passage set by the Scripture Union or Bible Reading Fellowship, in the
evening you can work slowly through a gospel or
epistle, or vice versa.

Now here are four suggestions as to how to read your
allotted portion:

1. *Pray!* Do not begin to read until you have
prayed. You cannot read the Bible with the casual
indifference which you might give to the newspaper.
The Bible is God's word. It must be approached
with that "reverence and humility without which no
man can understand Thy truth", as John Calvin said.
The purpose of reading the Bible is not just reading the
Bible. The purpose of Bible-reading is that through
it we may meet Christ. The Bible is His portrait. As
we gaze at Him in it, He can come alive and step from
the canvas and commune with us. If we are seeking
the living Word (Christ) through the written word (the
Bible), we shall need to read unhurriedly and atten-
tively. It will not be enough to say a prayer before we
read; we shall read in a prayerful attitude of mind.

2. *Think!* I am not suggesting that God will do all
the work, and that we have nothing to do. On the contrary, we must think as well as pray. "Think over what
I say, for the Lord will grant you understanding in
everything," wrote Paul to Timothy (2 Tim. 2: 7).
He will do the granting of understanding; but we must
do the thinking. We must combine our own researches
with dependence on the Holy Spirit's illumination. It
is very valuable to use the Revised Standard Version or

[1] The Scripture Union, 3–5 Wigmore Street, London W.1; The
Bible Reading Fellowship, 12 Buckingham Palace Gardens, London
S.W.1.

one of the modern paraphrases of the Bible, or a good commentary, to help us to understand the text of the Authorized Version. Even this, however, will not save us the bother of thinking hard ourselves. We must read, re-read and go on reading the passage. We must wrestle with its meaning. We must worry at it like a dog with a bone. We must meditate on it. We must ask first "What does the passage *mean?*" and then "What does it *say to me?*" Do not be content with an understanding of the passage. Go on to apply it in practical ways to the details of your own life and circumstances.

3. *Remember!* If God speaks to us, we must strive to remember what He says. A bad memory was the downfall of Israel. The people kept forgetting the lessons God had taught them. One great stimulus to the memory is a pen. Keep a notebook in which you can write down either by days, or under subject headings, or under books of the Bible, the special truths God teaches you. Then you will be able to look over them from time to time. Another way is to learn by heart exceptionally helpful verses. Make a list of them and keep revising them. If you commit to memory one verse a week, with its reference, your knowledge of God and His word will steadily develop.

4. *Obey!* It is little use reading the Bible at all if we never put it into practice. To pray and think and remember are wasted effort if we disobey what we learn. Jesus said that the wise man who built his house on the rock was someone who heard His sayings and did them. James, too, appeals to us to be doers and not just hearers of the word. He likens the Bible to a mirror, and rather sarcastically describes a disobedient Bible-reader as someone who looks in the mirror, sees that he needs to wash his face or brush his hair, and then immediately forgets to do it!

2. PRAYER

Rightly understood, prayer is always a response to God's word. God speaks first (through the Bible). Our answer is prayer. If this is so, my first piece of advice to you is this. If God speaks to you from your portion on some particular subject, begin by talking back to Him on the same subject. To do so is only polite. Do not change the conversation! Keep your Bible open before you and go through your passage again, verse by verse, turning it into prayer. You will find this a great joy. It will also help you to translate what you have read into your everyday life.

When you have done this, you will want to go on to pray in other ways. Be as natural as possible. God is your Heavenly Father. He wants you to talk to Him about everything. A middle-aged cook in one of the Government Ministries said to me recently: "I find you can talk to God kind of confidential-like. You can tell 'Im some of your secrets—just between you and 'Im alone!" She was quite right. At the same time, do not be afraid of using set forms of prayer instead of, or as well as, your own words which you make up. Many people find this a help. There are several good books of prayers available. Or you can gradually make up your own.

In order to ensure that our prayer-time has balance, it is good to remember that there are five different kinds of prayer, all of which should find a place in our devotions:

1. *The Look Up at God*. This is *worship*. It is giving God the glory which is due to His Name. It is also the best antidote in the world to self-centredness. An ancient writer called it the way to disinfect us of egotism. In true worship we turn the searchlight of our mind upon God. We forget our sinful and trouble-some selves for a few brief and welcome moments.

We think only of God and Christ and the Holy Spirit. We marvel at the beauties of creation and survey the wondrous cross on which the Prince of Glory died. We are just taken up with God. Jesus taught us to do this. The Lord's Prayer begins with concern for God's glory and not our own needs. We concentrate on the hallowing of *His* name, the spreading of *His* kingdom and the doing of *His* will. You will not find this easy at first. We are so turned in on ourselves, that it requires real mental contortions to turn our mind inside out before we can gaze and gaze on God. But persevere. Nothing is more right or more important. It may help your mind to concentrate if you say over slowly and thoughtfully some of the great objective hymns like "Holy, holy, holy", "My God, how wonderful Thou art" or "Immortal, invisible, God only wise".

2. *The Look In at Ourselves.* This leads to *confession*. Everybody knows that too much introspection is unhealthy and unhelpful; but some is very salutary. Much of our Bible-reading will sober us in this way. The word of God ruthlessly exposes our sin and selfishness, our greed and pride. Let God's word lead us to repentance and confession. It is also a most spiritually hygienic exercise each evening to look back carefully over the day and call to mind one's sins. Not to do so tends to make us slapdash and leads us to presume upon God's mercy; to make a habit of doing so will humble and shame us, and increase our longings for greater holiness. There is nothing morbid about this discipline, so long as after we have recalled our sins, we confess and forsake them, humbly ask and gratefully receive God's forgiveness, and then forget them. It is never unwise to look in, so long as you look out again quickly.

3. *The Look Round at our Friends.* This is *intercession*, or prayer for other people. Jesus prayed for

His disciples and for His enemies. St. Paul prayed for his converts and for the Churches God had used him to found. We, too, must remember our friends in prayer. It is the best service we can render them. Most Christians keep a prayer list. On it you will want to include your family and friends, your associates at work, your godchildren and relatives and the minister of your Church. Find room, too, to pray for your Queen and country, for the peace of the world and for the work of the Church at home and abroad, especially through any missionaries you may personally know. Obviously, if you are to remember all these people and needs (and others of your own that I have not mentioned) you will need a system of some kind. I suggest you work out your own, so that you pray for some people daily, others weekly and others only monthly or from time to time. Whatever system you have, keep it elastic and adaptable. One other point needs to be made here: do be specific in your prayers. Avoid vague requests for God's blessing. We must not be afraid to pray definitely for somebody's conversion, or growth in holiness, or that he may discover God's will for his career.

4. *The Look Back at the Past.* *Thanksgiving* differs from worship in that in worship we praise God for what He is in Himself, while in thanksgiving we thank Him for what He has done for us. Israel's forgetfulness led to ingratitude. The people had been told to remember all that God had done for them, but "they soon forgot His works" (Ps. 106: 13). I hope we shall not follow their example. "Bless the Lord, O my soul, and forget not all His benefits" (Ps. 103:2). The General Thanksgiving gives a wonderful summary of the many blessings of God for which we should give thanks to Him—"our creation, preservation and all the blessings of this life", God's inestimable love in redeeming the world through the Lord Jesus, all the means of grace

(the Bible, prayer, the Lord's Supper, Christian fellow-ship, etc.), and "the hope of glory" (that is, the cer-tainty that in His goodness we are going to heaven when we die). At the end of each day it is good to look back over it to recall not only our sins but God's mercies. If we confess the one, let us not forget to give thanks for the other.

5. *The Look On at the Future.* I have left *petition* or supplication to the last. What looms largest in the prayers of most of us is actually the least important of all. Yet petition should have a real place in our prayers. Jesus told us to ask our Heavenly Father to supply all our needs—physical ("give us this day our daily bread"), spiritual ("forgive us our trespasses") and moral ("deliver us from the evil one"); and St. Paul wrote that we were "in everything by prayer and supplication with thanksgiving" to let our "requests be made known to God" (Phil. 4 : 6). The purpose of such petition is neither to inform God of our needs, as if He were ignorant of them, nor to bully Him to meet them as if He were reluctant to do so. God is our Heavenly Father. He knows our needs before we ask, and in His love for us He longs to meet them. Then why should we pray? We need to pray for our sakes, rather than for His. We pray not in order to impose our wills on His will, but to align them to it. Our Father does not spoil His children. He does not lavish gifts on us which we do not want, nor force His will upon us. He waits until we desire His will; and prayer is the way by which we bring ourselves to do so. So every true petition is a variation on the grand theme "Thy will be done". We look ahead therefore into the future. We anticipate the duties and problems, the hopes and fears, of today and tomorrow and next week and next year. What is our wish? The Christian has only one: "Not my will but Thine be done". He asks therefore for guidance to know God's will, and for strength to do it.

The Christian life is a life of prayer, in that it is a life of communion with God through Christ; and the more disciplined the Christian is in his set times of quiet, the more easy he will find it to "pray without ceasing" (1 Thess. 5: 17), and to abide in Christ, enjoying His presence throughout every minute of each day.

QUESTIONS FOR GROUP DISCUSSION

1. What is the relation between revelation and reason?
2. What steps do you take to get the most out of your daily Bible-reading?
3. "Pray without ceasing." What do you think Paul meant by this command, and how can we obey it?

9

Fellowship and the Holy Communion

IF the first great secret of progress in the Christian life is daily times of Bible-reading and prayer, the second is the regular enjoyment of fellowship with other Christians. The Christian life is not to be lived in splendid isolation. You cannot sit in your corner like little Jack Horner and suck your thumb or eat plum pudding! That is not Christianity. "To turn Christianity into a solitary religion," said John Wesley, "is to destroy it." True, personal relationship to God is both possible and necessary, but to restrict religion to this is to make it hopelessly lopsided. The same Jesus who in His Sermon on the Mount gave advice about private prayer beginning "When thou prayest" (singular), added a few verses later "When ye pray" (plural) and continued "after this manner therefore pray ye: Our Father . . ." (Mt. 6: 5, 6, 7, 9).

God's purpose is not just to save independent souls, but to build a Church. The New Testament writers add simile to simile in painting their picture of it. It is a family in which we are all brothers and sisters, a kingdom in which we are fellow-citizens, and the body of Christ of which He is the Head and we the members. We are also sheep in the same flock under the same Shepherd, branches of the vine and stones in the building. It is impossible to escape from each other. We belong to each other as we belong to Him.

Not only is fellowship with other Christians a Christian duty; it is also a great help. The Church exerts a stabilizing influence on the Christian. Most

Christians pass through turbulent periods of doubt and difficulty. The fellowship will hold and steady you in these times. What would a boy or girl do, passing through the stormy years of adolescence, without the shelter and support of the family? Probably you are already a member of a local Church. If not, you must join one quickly. It is quite wrong to suppose that you can belong to the universal, invisible Church without belonging to its local, visible counterpart in the place where you live. And please do not become an ecclesiastical gypsy, with no fixed abode. Sermon-tasters are worse than pub-crawlers! Your confirmation means partly that you have become a full member of the Church of England. It would be ludicrous to receive both the privilege and the responsibility of membership and then enjoy neither.

I want to encourage you to make the very most of Christian fellowship. Do not rest content with mere attendance at Sunday services. Throw yourself body and soul into the Christian family. Go to at least one midweek meeting of your local Church if time permits—the prayer meeting, the Bible School, a club or a class. Be sure your *best* friends are Christians (though have plenty of friends who are not; you will want to win them for Christ). Try to meet your Christian friends during the week, and do not be shy of talking with them about spiritual things. Why not get a group of them together for informal Bible-reading and prayer once a week or fortnight? What could be more natural than for members of the same family to talk together to their Father? And speaking of Christian friends, be sure that your special boy friend or girl friend, if the time has come for you to have one, is a Christian too. Christians are at liberty to marry only Christians. Marriage is too wonderful and sacred a thing to be a unity that is physical, social and intellectual but not spiritual (2 Cor. 6: 14).

THE HOLY COMMUNION

The chief expression of fellowship between Christians is the Holy Communion service. It is the central service of the Church. It was instituted by the Lord Jesus Himself, and observed by the earliest Christians. The Acts of the Apostles suggests that every Sunday they met to "break bread". The Lord's Day was inconceivable without the Lord's Supper. Personally, I think we, too, should attend it every Sunday. We should certainly have a rule for regular attendance (fortnightly or monthly if not weekly) and stick to it without fail.

"The Lord's Supper" is still the main title which our Prayer Book gives the service ("Holy Communion" being the sub-title). It is St. Paul's expression (1 Cor. 11 : 20). It describes what it is—the fellowship meal of Christians by invitation of the Lord Jesus. The modern habit of having several Communion services every Sunday, thus splitting the congregation into segments, does not stimulate the sense of fellowship, although the "Family Communion" or "Parish Communion" is a step in the right direction. Straight and formal pews are not conducive to fellowship either, especially when members of the congregation go and sit as far as possible from each other as they can!

The Lord's Supper has other meanings apart from fellowship, and to these I must now come. I will restrict myself to the four major themes of the service. I think you would find it profitable to concentrate on one theme at a time when you attend the service.

1. *Remembrance.* The simplest and most obvious meaning of the Lord's Supper is that it commemorates the death of Jesus Christ on the cross. St. Paul has preserved the earliest account of the institution of the service (since the first epistle to the Corinthians was

written before the gospels). According to this, Jesus took bread and broke it, referred to it as His body, and said: "Do this in remembrance of me". Then He took the cup, called it "the new covenant in my blood", and said: "Do this, as often as you drink it, in remembrance of me" (1 Cor. 11: 24, 25). The actions of His hands and the words of His mouth combined to speak of His death. The Church has always recognized that the first and foremost purpose of the Communion service was by word and action to remind Christians of Christ's death. The third exhortation reads: "To the end that we should alway remember the exceeding great love of our Master and only Saviour Jesus Christ, thus dying for us, and the innumerable benefits which by His precious blood-shedding He hath obtained to us, He hath instituted and ordained holy mysteries, as pledges of His love, and for a continual remembrance of His death, to our great and endless comfort." More simply, the Catechism states that the sacrament of the Lord's Supper was ordained "for the continual remembrance of the sacrifice of the death of Christ, and of the benefits which we receive thereby".

So the officiating minister in the Prayer of Consecration copies the actions, and repeats the words, of Jesus. He takes bread and wine and places his hand over them to consecrate them. That is, he sets them apart from ordinary use to be special symbols of the body and blood of Christ. The Prayer Book rubric [1] says that the clergyman should perform the so-called "manual acts" (breaking the bread and taking the cup into his hands) "before the people". What he does should be visible to the congregation. Many people find it a help at this important point in the service to look up and watch, just as the disciples must have

[1] The "rubrics" are the instructions to minister and congregation which are printed in italics throughout the different services of the Prayer Book.

watched Jesus in the upper room. Think to yourself as you look and listen: "As that bread is being broken, so His body was given for me on the cross", and "the wine is being set apart to represent His blood which He shed for me".

2. *Participation.* Jesus did not only break the bread; He gave it to the disciples to eat. He did not only pour out the wine; He gave it to them to drink. He said not only "This is my body", "this is my blood", but "take, eat" and "drink this". He was not content that they should watch and listen; they must eat and drink. So the service is a communion as well as a commemoration. The congregation are not just spectators of a drama; they are partakers of a supper. Christ means us not only to remember His death, but also to share in its benefits by faith.

This is what St. Paul meant when he asked: "The cup of blessing which we bless, is it not a participation (or, communion) in the blood of Christ? The bread which we break, is it not a participation (or, communion) in the body of Christ?" (1 Cor. 10: 16). It is important to think clearly about this, because, alas! it has become a cause of division in the Church of Christ. Two questions confront us. First, *in what* do we participate? Secondly, *how* do we participate in it?

First, of what is the Lord's Supper a participation? Paul says it is a participation in the body and blood of Christ. But what are they? It is vital to understand that the expression "the body and blood of Christ" means Christ's death (and the benefits of His death). The Communion bread is broken; it stands for the body of Jesus not as it lived in Galilee or Judea, but as it was broken or given in death on the cross. The wine is poured out; it stands for the blood of Jesus not as it flowed in His veins while He lived, but as it was shed in death on the cross. So the body and blood

of Christ signify not Christ's life, but His death. It is
His loving purpose that we should share at Communion not in His life and its power, but in His death
and its benefits. He is presented to us in the Supper as
our crucified Saviour, who laid down His life for our
forgiveness.

Secondly, how do we partake of His body and
blood? We do not share in His body and blood simply
by eating the bread and drinking the wine. It is perfectly possible, as Article 29 makes clear, to eat and
drink at Communion and never receive Christ's body
and blood.[1] The Church of England does not believe
in transubstantiation, which is the supposed change of
the substance of the bread and wine into the substance
of the body and blood of Christ. No. Article XXVIII
(*Of the Lord's Supper*) perfectly answers our question:
"The Supper of the Lord is . . . a Sacrament of our
redemption by Christ's death: insomuch that to such
as rightly, worthily, and with faith, receive the same,
the bread which we break is a partaking of the Body of
Christ; and likewise the cup of blessing is a partaking
of the blood of Christ. . . . The body of Christ is
given, taken, and eaten, in the Supper, only after an
heavenly and spiritual manner. And the mean whereby
the Body of Christ is received and eaten in the Supper
is faith. . . ." The Catechism teaches the same truth
in saying: "The body and blood of Christ . . . are
verily and indeed taken and received by the faithful
(i.e. those who exercise faith) in the Lord's Supper."
Richard Hooker, in his "Laws of Ecclesiastical Polity"
summed it up by writing: "The real presence of
Christ's most blessed body and blood is not to be

[1] Article XXIX. *Of the wicked which eat not the Body of Christ
in the use of the Lord's Supper*. "The wicked, and such as be
void of a lively faith, although they do carnally and visibly press
with their teeth (as St. Augustine saith) the Sacrament of the
Body and Blood of Christ, yet in no wise are they partakers of
Christ. . . ."

sought for in the sacrament, but in the worthy receiver of the sacrament." [1]

So throughout the service there is something visible and something invisible. The visible minister represents the invisible Christ, who is the chief host at His supper and is really present at (but not on) His table. The visible minister offers visible bread and wine to our visible bodies; the invisible Christ offers His invisible body and blood (the forgiveness purchased by His death) to our invisible souls. How do our bodies receive the bread and wine offered by the minister? By eating and drinking. How do our souls receive the forgiveness of our sins offered us by Christ through His death? By faith, of which eating and drinking are the perfect physical equivalent. So the bread and wine are only symbols. Our eyes see the symbols; but our faith looks beyond the symbols to the reality for which they stand, and thankfully appropriates anew the precious body and blood of Christ. Nothing could be clearer than the actual words of administration. I may perhaps be permitted to amplify them in order to interpret their meaning: "Take and eat this (bread), in remembrance that Christ died for thee, and as thou dost feed on it in thy mouth by eating, so feed on Him in thy heart by faith."

3. *Fellowship*. We have already seen that the Lord's Supper is the centre of the Church's fellowship. It is described in Article XXVIII as "a sign of the love that Christians ought to have among themselves one to another". Five times in 1 Corinthians 11, in the space of eighteen verses, St. Paul uses the verb "to come together". The Lord's Supper is a gathering together of Christian people. Our Prayer Book still says that for Communion the Holy Table "shall stand in the body of the Church or in the Chancel". Our reformers meant the congregation to kneel round it like a family gathered

[1] "Ecclesiastical Polity", V, p. 67.

for a meal. This used to be the universal custom, and still takes place in a few churches. Even with the Communion Table at the east end of the church, however, our fellowship is not destroyed. We kneel side by side at the rail without distinction. The duchess and the daily, the mistress and her maid, father and son, master and pupil, man and wife, coloured and white, rich and poor. At the Lord's Table we are all one. This truth Paul sees hidden in the very bread we eat. "Because there is one loaf, we who are many are one body, for we all partake of the same loaf" (1 Cor. 10: 17). Each communicant receives a fragment from the same loaf because each is a member of the same body, the body of Christ, the Church. Indeed, there is a yet deeper meaning here. The loaf is an emblem of the crucified Saviour, and it is our common participation in Him (symbolized by our common participation in it) which makes us one. So the words of administration are very personal. "The body of our Lord Jesus Christ which was given for *thee* . . . Christ died for *thee* . . . Christ's blood was shed for *thee* . . ."; but as soon as the administration is over and we have returned to our pews, each personally assured of his blood-bought salvation, we say immediately together: "*Our* Father . . ."

4. *Thanksgiving.* From very early days the Lord's Supper has been called "the Eucharist", which is the Greek word for "thanksgiving". This may originally have been because Jesus "gave thanks" to God when He took the bread and wine. But the service is a "eucharist", too, because in it we give our thanks to God for Christ's wonderful love and death for us, for our share in the benefits of His death, and for our fellowship together which is based upon it.

It is in this sense that the Lord's Supper is, or includes, a "sacrifice". It is "this our sacrifice of praise and thanksgiving". When I was at school, I used to think that Holy Communion was a sacrifice, because I found it a great sacrifice to get up so early on Sunday mornings to attend it! But that is not what the words mean. A sacrifice is an offering; and in the service we offer to God our heartfelt gratitude for His mercy in the death of Jesus.

The Lord's Supper is not a sacrifice of Christ. We do not offer Christ to God in it. We remember Christ's sacrifice; we partake by faith of its benefits; we enjoy together the fellowship it made possible; but we do not in any sense repeat it or represent it. To do so, as our Anglican Reformers clearly saw, would be an insult to Christ and, as Bishop Nicholas Ridley wrote, "a great derogation of the merits of Christ's passion". At the beginning of the splendid Prayer of Consecration the minister says that Christ made on the cross "(by His one oblation of Himself once offered) a full, perfect, and sufficient sacrifice, oblation (*that is*, offering) and satisfaction, for the sins of the whole world". Article XXXI adds: "and there is none other satisfaction for sin, but that alone". Again, we do not sacrifice Christ in the consecrated elements at Communion, because He is not there under the forms of bread and wine to be offered. So too, strictly speaking, we have no altars in our churches, because an altar is a place of sacrifice. The word "altar" is not found in our Prayer Book. The reformers carefully and deliberately excluded it. They wrote instead of "the Holy Table", "the Lord's Table", "the Communion Table" or simply "the Table". The officiant at Communion is not a priest sacrificing at an altar; he is a minister serving at a table. He administers a sacrament to the people; he does not offer a sacrifice to God.

But the congregation offer a sacrifice to God in the body of the church. They offer themselves. They echo in their hearts the moving words of the Prayer of Oblation which follows the administration: "Here we offer and present unto Thee, O Lord, ourselves, our souls and bodies, to be a reasonable, holy, and lively sacrifice unto Thee . . . and although we be unworthy, through our manifold sins, to offer unto Thee any sacrifice, yet we beseech Thee to accept this our bounden duty and service . . ."

THE STRUCTURE OF THE SERVICE

There is a clear rhythm to be found in the structure of the Communion service, and a brief explanation of this may help you to understand the service better. It begins with our preparation of ourselves (called the antecommunion) leading up to the confession of our sins. Then, first through His word and then through the sacrament, God assures us of our forgiveness. We respond in thanksgiving and praise. Finally, He dismisses us with His blessing.

1. *Preparation.* The service begins with the Lord's Prayer, which is said by the minister alone. This is all that is left of the priest's elaborate self-preparation in the medieval services. The best thing to do as the minister says this prayer is to pray for him. The Collect for Purity follows, in which we pray that our worship may be sincere and true. Then the preparation of the congregation begins. It is assumed that each communicant will prepare himself privately before he comes. "Let a man examine himself, and so eat of the bread and drink of the cup," wrote St. Paul (1 Cor. 11: 28). Yet the service continues our private preparation with a public one. "What is required of them who come to the Lord's Supper?" asks the last question in the Catechism. *Answer*: "To examine themselves, whether they *repent* them truly of their former sins, stedfastly purposing to lead a new life; have a lively *faith* in God's mercy through Christ, with a thankful remembrance of His death; and be in *charity* with all men." The words in italics point to the three condi-

tions on which we may receive that forgiveness of God for which we come to the Lord's Supper. They are repentance, faith and love. So the antecommunion gives us the opportunity publicly to fulfil these conditions.

(a) *Repentance*. The ten commandments are read. Or sometimes Christ's summary of the law is used instead. After each commandment we say "Lord, have mercy upon us (forgiving us for our transgression of it in the past) and incline our hearts to keep this law" (in the future). Thus do we prepare ourselves by repentance. The prayer for the Queen follows, probably because it would be impossible to keep God's commandments without an ordered society.

(b) *Faith*. The collect, epistle and gospel for the day are then read. Through these we hear God's word (which is then sometimes expounded in a sermon), and we make our response in the creed, "I believe . . ." Thus is our faith in God's mercy awakened and declared.

(c) *Love*. The offertory follows. Communion alms are always given to the sick and poor. Then comes the Prayer for the Church Militant, in which we pray for the rulers of the nations, our Queen and those in authority under her, ministers of the gospel, all Christian people and especially the present congregation, and all in trouble and adversity. Thus, by our gifts and our prayers, do we express our love.

Only then does the minister give the Invitation: "Ye that do truly and earnestly *repent* you of your sins, and are in *love* and charity with your neighbours . . . draw near with *faith* . . ."

2. *Communion*. After this careful preparation and this solemn invitation, we confess our sins to God, minister and people together. We are now reaching the heart of the service. God purposes to give His penitent and believing people, who are in love and

charity with all men, the assurance of His forgiveness.
He does so in two ways:

(a) *By His word.* The minister says the Absolution,
expressing God's promise to forgive those who heartily
repent and truly believe. This he endorses by the
"comfortable words", four of the greatest gospel texts
in the Bible. Open your ears and your heart. Drink in
these messages of grace. Let them quieten your conscience and reassure your heart. These words of divine
assurance are followed by a preliminary thanksgiving
which include the *Sursum Corda* ("Lift up your
hearts") and the *Sanctus* ("Holy, holy, holy . . .").

(b) *By His sacrament.* God is not content to pledge
His forgiveness to us by audible words; He adds a
visible sign. The minister first says the beautiful
Prayer of Humble Access and then consecrates bread
and wine to exhibit symbolically Christ's body and
blood given for our salvation. These we come forward to eat and to drink. They are emblems of His
dying love. They are tokens of His forgiveness. They
endorse the promise of His words.

3. *Thanksgiving.* Returning to our seats, we join
together in the Family Prayer. Then follows the
Prayer of Oblation in which we offer ourselves, our
souls and bodies, as a sacrifice to God, or the alterna-
tive prayer in which we thank God that He has both
fed us "with the spiritual food of the most precious
body and blood" of Christ and also assured us that we
are forgiven sinners, members of His Church and heirs
of His everlasting kingdom. Next comes the *Gloria
in Excelsis*, a very ancient expression of worship to
the Heavenly King and the Lamb of God.

4. *Blessing.* So the service ends. We have prepared
ourselves in repentance, faith and love. God has
assured us of His forgiveness by word and sign. We
have praised and worshipped Him for His grace. But
we do not leave church with words upon our own lips.

The last word is God's, as through the lips of His minister He promises us His peace which passes all understanding. It is for this that we have come to the Lord's Supper. It is this that we have received from His word and sacrament—peace of mind and conscience and heart.

QUESTIONS FOR GROUP DISCUSSION

1. "I'm a perfectly good Christian, but I don't go to church." Discuss this statement.
2. Why did Jesus institute the Lord's Supper?
3. How can we best prepare ourselves to come to the Holy Communion service?

10

The Service of Christ

Paul and Peter, James and Jude all begin their epistles by describing themselves as "a slave of Jesus Christ". What they were, we are. Every Christian is Jesus Christ's slave. The reason for this is not far to seek. "You are not your own; you were bought with a price" (1 Cor. 6: 19, 20). We have exchanged one slavery for another. We were the slaves of sin and self; but Jesus Christ has liberated us. He has bought us in the slave-market. His precious blood was the price He paid to ransom us. So now we belong to Him. We have no rights of our own. We are His bondservants. As such we owe Him an unquestioning obedience and an ungrudging service, and, as one of the collects rightly says, we shall find His service to be perfect freedom.

There are two main ways in which we can serve Jesus Christ.

1. WORK

Everybody is a worker. Nobody can live without working. But the quality of the Christian's work should be far better than even the most conscientious unbeliever's, simply because he has learned to work so as to please his heavenly Master.

This principle applies universally. Whether you are a boy or girl at school, a student at the university, a housewife at home, a man or woman earning your living, if you are a committed Christian, your daily work can and should be service for Jesus Christ. It is a

great mistake to suppose that your service for Him
is your spare-time Christian activity and that the day's
work is merely a dismal drudgery or the wearisome
business of breadwinning. To separate your Christian
life into two compartments like this is asking for
trouble, and is thoroughly dishonouring to Jesus Christ.
He is our Master and we are His slaves all day long
seven days a week, and we must learn to do everything
we do as part of our service for Him. Of course there
are some kinds of employment in which a Christian
cannot stay. Provided your work is honourable, however, and it is God's will for you, then "whatever your
task, work heartily, as serving the Lord, and not men"
(Col. 3 : 23). If you are still at school or college, I urge
you to work hard for Christ. Multitudes of men and
women look back to their schooldays and wish they had
worked harder. These years of educational opportunity
will never come again. Christians ought to be known in
the school or university, whether they have brains or
not, for their good honest slogging and for their trust-
worthiness in positions of responsibility.

The same principle continues to hold good when you
go out into the world. I am not giving advice to school-
children but to *Christians*. Working for Christ is
just as urgent a duty for adult men and women. If
you are a girl, and God gives you the privilege of
marriage and a family, then obviously your Christian
work is in your home—looking after your husband and
caring for your children. Christian mothers are about
the most influential people in the world. Your prayers,
example and teaching can bring your children naturally
and easily to trust and serve the Lord Jesus. But they
must be able to see Him in you.

If you are an unmarried woman or a man, you will of
course spend much of your time earning your living.
Remember then that a Christian's incentives to work
are not the same as a non-Christian's. I do not mean

in any way to despise worldly incentives. A congenial job, a fair wage, reasonable hours, good conditions, decent holidays and a pension are quite certainly pleasing to God. But I hope that a Christian can see beyond his job and his Friday night pay-packet. For one thing, he will see his family, for whose sake he is earning. He will also think of his country, which depends for its stable economy largely on the industry of its citizens. A Christian will look further still than this. He will see himself in his daily work as fulfilling a divine purpose.

Let me put it like this. Every human being has been put on probation by God. This life is a probationary period. God's purpose for us while we are on earth is that we should turn to Jesus Christ as our Saviour and Lord, and then through Him grow into balanced, healthy, active, useful, happy, holy people. The development of spiritual personality is God's will for our lives. Now for the fulfilment of His purpose He has humbled Himself to depend on our co-operation. When a baby is born into this world, he is not able to develop on his own. He needs parents to care for him, teachers to educate his mind and doctors to keep his body healthy. He needs facilities for recreation. He cannot do without food, clothing, shelter or an ordered society in which to live. Every honourable employment, in one of the professions, in business, industry or commerce, fits somewhere into this picture. Every Christian can see himself working hand in hand with God. He can have no greater incentive than to know that he is collaborating with Christ. So he can learn to do his job "as to the Lord and not unto men". If you are an employee, look beyond your boss to Jesus Christ your Master. If you are an employer or self-employed, remember that you also have an Employer in heaven. George Herbert expresses this admirably in his hymn:

Teach me, my God and King,
    In all things Thee to see;
And what I do in anything
    To do it as for Thee.

All may of Thee partake;
    Nothing can be so mean
Which, with this tincture, for Thy sake,
    Will not grow bright and clean.

A servant with this clause
    Makes drudgery divine;
Who sweeps a room, as for Thy laws,
    Makes that and the action fine.

This is the famous stone
    That turneth all to gold;
For that which God doth touch and own
    Cannot for less be told.

There is one other point to mention before I pass
on. It is this. So far I have assumed that you are
engaged in what we usually call "secular employment".
Of course for a Christian no employment is really
secular; he views it as spiritual and as part of his
service for Jesus Christ. At the same time, there are
other spheres of service which are yet more directly
concerned with the spread of the kingdom of God on
earth. I am thinking particularly of the ordained
ministry and the mission-field. There is a very
great need in both spheres today. Sheer lack of
man-power in these directions is hindering the
Church's advance. Cosmo Gordon Lang, formerly
Archbishop of Canterbury, used to say that there
should come a time in every young man's life when he
asks himself *not* "Is there any reason why I should
enter the ministry?" *but* "Is there any reason why I
should not?" Do keep your mind open and your will
surrendered to this possibility. There is no greater

privilege on earth than preaching the gospel of Jesus Christ and doing the other tasks allotted to ministers and missionaries. It is work which even angels may not do. If you are beginning to consider these things at all, I advise you to consult your vicar as soon as possible.

2. WITNESS

Although not every Christian is called to the mission-field or into the ministry, every Christian is called to be a witness. It is the second part of his bondservice to Jesus Christ.

The strange idea is current today that Christians are a bunch of selfish prigs, too concerned about their own salvation to bother much about anybody else. I am afraid there is some justification for this criticism. Some of us are so keen to develop our own spiritual lives, and to enjoy Christian fellowship, that we neglect our responsibility to those still outside. But if the Christian has a duty to God and to the Church, he has a duty to the world as well.

This duty is to be a witness to Jesus Christ, and to seek by every available means to spread to others the saving knowledge of his Lord and Saviour. His con-firmation includes this task. Confirmation has been called "the ordination of the laity". When the Bishop lays his hand on your head, it is not only to assure you of God's blessing but to commission you to go forth into the world as a witness to Jesus Christ. I under-stand that a diocese of China has added to the three vows in the Confirmation service a fourth which reads: "I will win to the Christian Church one person each year." St. Paul went so far as to say that if his converts were not "holding forth the word of life" to others, he would regard his labour as having been in vain (Phil. 2: 15).

Not only does the Bible teach us that evangelism is a duty resting upon every Christian, but the situation in the Church today demands it. The population is growing. The number of ministers is decreasing. The gulf between the Churches and the masses is widening. Tens of thousands of our fellow-countrymen are not only indifferent to the way of salvation in Jesus Christ, but actually ignorant of it. Who is going to reach them? Not the parson. He is too scarce a commodity. He is also far too busy with other ministerial duties to visit everybody in his parish. Besides, many people in factory and shop and office are out of his reach. Then who is going to reach them? You! The ordinary Christian layman, as workmate or business colleague or neighbour, has opportunities to reach these folk with the gospel which are denied to the clergyman. If only *every* Christian were an active agent for the propagation of the gospel, and *every* Church a centre of virile and continuous evangelism, the whole country could be captured for Christ in a couple of decades. Awake, Christians!

But how can the Christian layman, the amateur missionary, witness to Christ and share in the evangelistic work of the Church? Here are six ways in which we can help:

(a) *By our prayers.* I have already written about intercession. Prayer is the secret of power. There is little hope of melting hard hearts if they have not first been softened by prayer.

(b) *By our example.* We can talk till we are blue in the face, but our words will have little effect if what we say is contradicted by what we are. Young people, your parents will not be impressed by your desire to be confirmed, if you are still as untidy and thoughtless as ever. "Let your light so shine before men," said Jesus, "that they may see your good works (not hear your fine sermons) and give glory to your Father who

is in heaven" (Mt. 5 : 16). The witness of our lips will
be of small value if it is not corroborated by the example
of our lives. Let Christ first make us humble and un-
selfish, curb our tempers and control our tongues, and
our friends will be more ready to listen to what we have
to say. There is also little more influential in the
neighbourhood than the influence of a consecrated
Christian home, from which radiate love, joy and peace.

(c) *By our personal testimony*. I suggest that you ask
the Lord Jesus to lay on your heart a burden for just
one particular friend whom He wants you to try to win
for Him. He will probably guide you to someone of
your own sex and roughly your own age. Then concentrate on him. Woo his friendship. You are more
likely to win his soul once you have won his heart.
Do not just love his soul; love *him*. Be in no hurry.
Pray for him regularly and earnestly. Be tactful,
discreet and courteous. Spend time with him. Soon
you will be able to take him with you to church and to
other places where he will hear the gospel preached,
and perhaps to lend him a book or a booklet about
Christ. All the time be waiting patiently and prayer-
fully for an opportunity to tell him humbly and simply
what Christ means to you. In case he goes on then to
ask you how he can become a Christian, be prepared.
You might find it helpful to have clearly in your mind
the steps I have listed in Chapter 1 and to learn the
most important texts by heart, so that you can find
them quickly in your Bible and show them to him.
Persevere in urgent prayer and humble witness until
he has committed himself to Christ.

(d) *By our church work*. Every Church member
ought to be in some way or other a Church worker.
The Church is not like a bus, with the minister at the
wheel and a congregation of dozing passengers behind
him. It is an army with every soldier fighting and a
tug-of-war team in which every member is pulling his

weight. Your vicar will be able to tell you innumerable practical jobs which need to be done. There is cleaning the church, arranging the flowers, cooking and catering and washing up, addressing envelopes and licking stamps, carpentry and painting, sewing and mending, and a host of other things besides. Then, too, there are yet more responsible tasks—teaching in the Sunday School, helping in a Bible class, visiting in the parish, singing in the choir and serving on committees. The Holy Spirit endows different Christians with different gifts. Try to discover in what direction your talent lies, and then offer your services. If you do not feel qualified for such Christian service, ask your vicar to give you and your friends a course of special training. You will be sharing in the corporate witness and work of the Church; and whatever your job, in the limelight or behind the scenes, do be conscientious. Be a man or woman on whose word and work your vicar can completely rely.

(e) *By our gifts.* The Church's work at home and abroad is hamstrung by lack of funds. The general level of our Christian giving needs everywhere to rise, not only to keep pace with inflation, but also to honour God and help on His work. The freewill offering of our money is a symptom of the joyful dedication of ourselves to Christ. The Jews gave to God a tithe (one tenth) of their income; the Christian should certainly not give less. Let our giving be systematic, sacrificial and thoughtful, and remember: "God loves a cheerful giver" (2 Cor. 9: 7).

(f) *By our service in the community.* From the beginning of the Christian era, Christians have pioneered the way in social service—in teaching the young, nursing the sick, freeing slaves and reforming conditions in factories and prisons. Much of this work has now been taken over by the Government; but there are **very many opportunities left for Christians to help in** the voluntary social services—in youth clubs, prison visiting, the care of old people, moral welfare, school care committees and so on. There is a great need, too, for Christians to take their part in the important work of local government. Finally, we need to pray that God will give some of His people today new visions to suit new challenges. The Welfare State cannot possibly cater adequately for everybody. There are still many square pegs in round holes. There are great social needs and ills which are crying out for daring Christian thought and sacrificial Christian love—the condition of the mentally sick, vagrants, alcoholics, prostitutes and many others. May God demonstrate in our day the healing power of Christian love! It is our calling to love. It is also a forceful testimony to the source of our love, the Lord Jesus Himself.

*   *   *   *

Here, then, is the balance of the Christian life. My prayer is that every confirmation candidate, having begun to tread the Christian way by wholehearted, personal commitment to Jesus Christ, may bring honour to his Lord and Saviour by his deepening Christian belief and his shining Christian behaviour.

QUESTIONS FOR GROUP DISCUSSION

1. What ways and means can you devise to relate Christianity to your job?
2. What do you consider to be the three priority conditions of successful personal evangelism?
3. Make a list of the tasks you think laymen should be given to do in the Church.

A SHORT GUIDE TO THE DUTIES OF
CHURCH MEMBERSHIP

All baptized and confirmed members of the Church must play their full part in its life and witness. That you may fulfil this duty, we call upon you:

To follow the example of Christ in home and daily life, and to bear personal witness to Him.

To be regular in private prayer day by day.

To read the Bible carefully.

To come to church every Sunday.

To receive the Holy Communion faithfully and regularly.

To give personal service to Church, neighbours and community.

To give money for the work of parish and diocese and for the work of the Church at home and overseas.

Geoffrey Cantuar:
Cyril Ebor:
1954

Issued by the Archbishops of Canterbury and York.

SOME PRAYERS

1. *For those preparing to be confirmed.*

Look down, O Lord, in Thy fatherly goodness upon all those who are preparing themselves for confirmation. May they turn to Thy Son, Jesus Christ, in simple repentance, faith and surrender. Grant that what they thus secretly possess they may then openly profess, so that, having received Thy Holy Spirit into their hearts by the hearing of faith, they may be assured thereof by the laying-on of hands, and go forth strengthened by Thy grace to serve Thee in the fellowship of Thy Church and of Thy Son, Jesus Christ our Lord.

2. *For those who lack assurance.*

O Lord Jesus Christ, who didst invite the heavy laden to come to Thee, and didst promise to give them rest and never to cast them out, help us so to come to Thee that we may find rest in Thee, and so to believe Thy promise that we may know that Thou hast received us, for the glory of Thy Name, who with the Father and the Holy Spirit art ever worthy to be trusted and adored.

3. *For perseverance in the Christian life.*

O Lord God, when Thou givest to Thy servants to endeavour any great matter, grant us also to know that it is not the beginning, but the continuing of the same, until it be thoroughly finished, which yieldeth the true glory, through Him that for the finishing of Thy work laid down His life, our Redeemer, Jesus Christ.

(Sir Francis Drake, 1587, on the day he sailed into Cadiz.)

4. *For courage to be fully committed to the service of God.*

O God our Father, who didst not spare Thine only Son, delivering Him up for us all, save us from our sinful selfishness and fears. Move us by the constraint of Thy love to present our bodies a living sacrifice unto Thee, which is our reasonable service. Help us never to be ashamed to serve and obey Thee with all our hearts, in the midst of a world which neither knows nor honours Thee, through Him who loved us and gave Himself for us, Thy Son, Jesus Christ our Saviour.

5. *For growth in Christian understanding.*

O Lord, Heavenly Father, in whom is the fulness of light and wisdom, enlighten our minds by Thy Holy Spirit, and give us grace to receive Thy word with reverence and humility, without which no man can understand Thy truth, for Christ's sake.

(John Calvin.)

6. *For holiness of life.*

O God, the God of all goodness and of all grace, who art worthy of a greater love than we can either give or understand, fill our hearts, we beseech Thee, with such love toward Thee, that nothing may seem too hard for us to do or to suffer in obedience to Thy will; and grant that thus loving Thee we may become daily more like unto Thee, and finally obtain the crown of life which Thou hast promised to those that love Thee; through Jesus Christ our Lord.

(Nineteenth-century Farnham Hostel Manual.)

7. *For the reading of the Bible.*

Almighty and most merciful God, who hast given the Bible to be the revelation of Thy great love to man, and of Thy power and will to save him: grant that our study of it may not be made in vain by the callousness or carelessness of our hearts; but that by it we may be confirmed in penitence, lifted to hope, made strong in service, and above all filled with the true knowledge of Thee and of Thy Son Jesus Christ.

(George Adam Smith.)

8. *For help in learning to pray.*

Our heavenly Father, who through Thy Son Jesus Christ hast said that men ought always to pray and not to faint, we beseech Thee, teach us to pray. Our spirit is willing but our flesh is weak. Give us grace each day to approach Thy throne and seek Thy face; to be concerned as much for Thy glory as for our need; and in everything by prayer and supplication with thanksgiving to make our requests known to Thee, until all our lives be gathered up into Thy presence and every breath is prayer, through Jesus Christ Thy Son, our ransom and our mediator.

9. *For our own local Church.*

O Lord Jesus Christ, who didst build Thy Church on the rock, that even the gates of hell might not prevail against it, have mercy on the Churches of this land, and especially on our own Church of .... Make the worship of our people acceptable in Thy sight; sweeten our fellowship with brotherly love; and unite us all in a continuous, bold, effective witness to our whole parish, for the spread of Thy kingdom and the glory of Thy holy Name.

10. *For a growing appreciation of the Holy Communion service.*

Lord Jesus Christ, we humbly thank Thee that Thou didst choose bread and wine to be the emblems of Thy sacred body and blood, given on the cross for the sins of the world, and didst command us thus to remember Thee. Deepen our repentance, strengthen our faith and increase our love for the brethren, that, eating and drinking the sacrament of our redemption, we may truly feed on Thee in our hearts with thanksgiving, for the sake of Thy great and worthy Name.

11. *For our daily work.*

O Lord Jesus Christ, who at the carpenter's bench didst manifest the dignity of honest labour, and dost give to each of us our tasks to perform, help us to do our weekday work with readiness of mind and single-ness of heart, not with eye-service as menpleasers, but as Thy servants, labouring heartily as unto Thee and not unto men, so that whatever we do, great or small, may be to the glory of Thy holy Name.

12. *For our witness to Jesus Christ.*

O God, who hast made man's mouth and canst cause even the dumb to speak, open our lips, we beseech Thee, that we may show forth Thy praise. Forgive us for our slow and stammering speech. Cause the fires to burn in our hearts until we can no longer hold our peace. Grant that, through our humble testimony to Thy Son Jesus Christ, our friends and neighbours may turn to Him as their Saviour and Lord, and magnify Him with us, in the fellowship of His Church, for the greater glory of His Name.